MW00436624

BIDEN
TIME

in his own words

COMPILED BY MIKE TOWLE

BIDEN TIME

Published by WND Books, Washington, D.C. WND Books is a registered trademark of WorldNetDaily.com, Inc. ("WND")

Book designed by Mark Karis
WND Books are available at special discounts for bulk purchases. WND Books also publishes books in electronic formats. For more information call (541) 474-1776 or visit www.wndbooks.com.

Paperback ISBN: 978-1-938067-96-9
eBook ISBN: 978-1-938067-97-6

Library of Congress Cataloging-in-Publication Data Available

Printed in the United States of America
14 15 16 17 18 19 LSI 9 8 7 6 5 4 3 2 1

This book is full of nearly unbelievable words spoken by a veritable politician. In order to prove that we aren't making this up, use your smartphone to scan the square codes to see video clips of Joe Biden actually saying some of these outlandish quotes as well as published articles that offer a record of his nonesense in perpetuity. To view all the videos in this book from your computer go to
YOUTUBE.COM/USER/THEWNDTV1

Download the **Scan** app on your smartphone for free. Then, open the app, point the camera at the code, and you're done! No need to take a photo or press a "scan" button.

*In order to use **Scan**, your device must have a built-in camera. When scanning codes that redirect to online content (such as websites), you will need Internet connectivity.

Download **Scan** on your smartphone today.

CONTENTS

INTRODUCTION

When Joe Biden steps up to a live microphone, it's like the green flag going down at the start of one of those local short-track stock car races—you never know when the first wreck is coming.

Public officials misspeaking during a public event or on a live television or radio interview is not that uncommon, but Biden has turned verbal goofs and gaffes into a modern art form. It sometimes comes complete with profane outbursts presumably not meant for public consumption; crass and even creepy talk apparently intended for mass distribution; and all sorts of other verbal bloopers, bleeps, and blunders. All this has made this American vice president as exasperating as he is at times endearing; as vexing as he is verbose.

Over the years, Biden has been burdened by charges of plagiarism and a reputation for laziness dating back to his academically challenging days at the University of Delaware and, later, Syracuse University School of Law. Those who know him have described Biden as an engaging guy who's a gab master of the sort of BS that would seemingly play better at frat parties, reunion gatherings, and lawn socials than in the sacred and polished halls of the US Capitol.

Biden Time offers a collection of hundreds of the most memorable and mystifying quotes by and about Biden dating back to when he was a lad growing up first in Scranton, Pennsylvania, and later in Wilmington, Delaware, all the time brandishing that familiar thousand-watt smile opposite that single-watt mental agility at the mic.

Expect to be entertained and humored by reading this book, which focuses on the lighter-weight side of Biden not likely to be prominently featured in his vice presidential library or in any of the high-achievement annals comprising the history of the Democratic Party. Biden served thirty-six years as a US Senator (D-DE) and at this writing appeared headed toward completing two terms and eight years as President Barack Obama's VP sidekick. For that he should be commended and command respect and our gratitude.

That said, let's now get on with, using one of his favorite expressions, all the "malarkey" that has over the years tumbled out of his mouth.

—MIKE TOWLE

TOP 25 BIDENISMS

Joe Biden is a big sports guy, a former high school and college jock, so he can appreciate this—kicking off this book with a top 25 list of his best lines, most memorable for the wrong reasons and in no particular order. There are plenty of top ten or top seven (or whatever) lists of classic Biden quotes floating around the Internet, but those lists don't do justice to his body of work when it comes to foot in mouth. The hard part was stopping at twenty-five for the sake of this opening salvo of solecism.

"I mean, you got the first mainstream African-American who is articulate and bright and clean and a nice-looking guy. I mean, that's a storybook, man."

The only story to be booked here were the headlines Biden generated with this forehead-slapping, politically incorrect assessment of Barack Obama near the beginning of the 2008 presidential primary campaign season (*New York Observer*, 2007). At the time, Biden and Obama were Democratic primary opponents. After this went viral, who would have thought that Obama about eighteen months later would pick Biden as his 2008 running mate?

VIDEO

"You cannot go to a 7-11 or a Dunkin Donuts unless you have a slight Indian accent. . . . I'm not joking."

Not joking? Well, as tennis great John McEnroe was so fond of saying, you cannot be serious! Biden said this during the 2006 C-SPAN series "Road to the White House" (*National Journal*/C-SPAN, July 6, 2006) while speaking with an Indian-American man and boasting about his support among Indian-Americans. To Biden's credit, at least he's always been willing to speak off the cuff and without use of a teleprompter, unlike his presidential boss Barack Obama.

VIDEO

"When the stock market crashed, Franklin D. Roosevelt got on the television and didn't just talk about the, you know, the princes of greed. He said, 'Look, here's what happened.'"

Okay, so perhaps Biden skipped school on the day they taught US history. Biden apparently didn't know that it was Herbert Hoover who was president when the stock market crashed in 1929; FDR took office in 1933. Only experimental TV sets were around at that time (CBS Evening News, Katie Couric interview, September 22, 2008).

VIDEO

"When seagull droppings landed on my head at a campaign event at Bowers Beach two days before Election Day, I chose to read it as a sign of a coming success."

Now that's looking at life through rose-colored glasses, although wouldn't it be easier, and cleaner, to read tea leaves if it's your future you want to know? (Biden, *Promises to Keep*, 73)

"His mom lived in Long Island for ten years or so. God rest her soul. And, although, she's . . . wait, your mom's still, your mom's still alive? Your dad passed. God bless her soul."

Biden speaking, during a March 2010 White House ceremony, about the mother of Irish Prime Minister Brian Cowen, who, it turns out, was very much alive (About.com).

VIDEO

"A man I'm proud to call my friend. A man who will be the next president of the United States—Barack America!"

Biden spoke with Barack Obama at a campaign rally in Springfield, Illinois, after he was announced as Obama's running mate. So this might not have been a gaffe; Obama, you might remember, did win a Nobel Prize soon after taking office. Maybe now we can believe in years to come that folks will look back thinking that our country was named after this guy (About.com).

VIDEO

"Look, John's last-minute economic plan does nothing to tackle the number-one job facing the middle class, and it happens to be, as Barack says, a three-letter word: jobs. J-O-B-S, jobs."

Biden fumbling basic math while speaking in Athens, Ohio, about 2008 Republican presidential candidate John McCain (About.com).

VIDEO

"I'm told Chuck Graham, state senator, is here. Stand up Chuck, let 'em see you. Oh, God love you. What am I talking about? I'll tell you what. You're making everybody else stand up, though, pal."

Telling Missouri paraplegic state senator Chuck Graham to stand up at a campaign rally, before realizing that Graham is confined to a wheelchair (*Time*, Sept. 9, 2008).

VIDEO

"I promise you, the president has a big stick.

I promise you."

Leave it to Biden to combine a double entendre with a racial stereotype in the space of twelve words (About.com), citing Theodore Roosevelt's famous quote, "Speak softly and carry a big stick; you will go far."

VIDEO

"If we do everything right, if we do it with absolute certainty, there's still a 30 percent chance we're going to get it wrong."

Addressing members of the House Democratic caucus gathered in Williamsburg, Virginia, in 2009 for their annual retreat (About.com).

VIDEO

"Now, people when I say that look at me and say, 'What are you talking about, Joe? You're telling me we have to go spend money to keep from going bankrupt?' The answer is yes, that's what I'm telling you."

Biden telling AARP town hall meeting attendees (CNS News, July 16, 2009) that unless the Democrat-supported health care plan becomes law, the nation will go bankrupt, and the only way to avoid that fate is for the government to spend more money. Nothing like foolish fear tactics to gain support for a bill that more than half of America never wanted.

VIDEO

"Hillary Clinton is as qualified or more qualified than I am to be vice president of the United States of America."

There you have it: Biden at a Nashua, New Hampshire, rally essentially admitting that Obama's former 2008 presidential primary rival, Senator Hillary Clinton, might have been a better choice for the vice president than him (CBS News, September 10, 2008).

VIDEO

"I guess what I'm trying to say without boring you too long at breakfast—and you all look dull as hell, I might add. The dullest audience I have ever spoken to. Just sitting there, staring at me. Pretend you like me!"

Teasing while trying half-heartedly to inspire a crowd of Turkish-American and Azerbaijani-American Obama donors (*New York Post*, April 27, 2012).

"I would tell members of my family, and I have, I wouldn't go anywhere in confined places right now. It's not that it's going to Mexico; it's that you are in a confined aircraft. When one person sneezes, it goes everywhere through the aircraft. That's me."

Sound the red alert! This is what Biden said when asked on NBC's *Today Show* (content.time.com) what he would tell his relatives if they wanted to fly to Mexico the next week. Scrambling for higher ground, White House press secretary Robert Gibbs later explained, "If people felt unduly alarmed for whatever reason, we would certainly apologize for that."

VIDEO

"Neal Smith, an old butt buddy. Are you here, Neal? Neal, I miss you man. I miss you."

We're not sure what conclusions we're supposed to jump to here, but we'll give Biden the benefit of the doubt that Neal Smith was just a good friend of his from bygone days. It's possible that Biden was having a brief reoccurrence of a stuttering problem that plagued him as a youth and that bud-buddy came out sounding like "butt buddy." But to this day the "butt buddy" remains one of the most mentioned when referring to Biden's propensity for verbal gaffes and blunders. For the record, at the time this was said, Biden was referring to Neal Smith, a ninety-four-year-old former Iowa congressman who was a Biden pal when he was in the Senate (*New York Post*, February 12, 2015).

VIDEO

"Romney wants to let the—he said in the first hundred days he's going to let the big banks once again write their own rules, 'unchain Wall Street.' They're going to put y'all back in chains."

Criticizing 2012 Republican presidential nominee Mitt Romney, his running mate Paul Ryan, and the Republican Party during a campaign speech in Danville, Virginia, before an audience that included many African Americans (*Washington Post*, 2012).

VIDEO

"Folks, I can tell you I've known eight presidents, three of them intimately."

Hmmmm (*Examiner*, 2012).

VIDEO

"Isn't it a bitch, this vice president thing?"

Biden speaking during a presentation at Harvard University, addressing a student who had identified himself as student body vice president, eliciting laughs from the audience. Biden quickly added that he was only kidding: "That was a joke. That was a joke. Best decision I ever made" (*Harvard Gazette*, 2014).

VIDEO

"You know, I'm embarrassed. Do you know the Web site number? I should have it in front of me, and I don't. I'm actually embarrassed."

Biden speaking to an aide standing out of view during an interview on CBS's *Early Show* (February 25, 2009). In the segment, he was telling viewers about a government-run Web site that tracks stimulus spending.

"Tonight, I want to acknowledge—I want to acknowledge, as we should every night, the incredible debt we owe to the families of those 6,473 fallen angels."

In standard parlance referring to spiritual matters, the expression "fallen angels" usually connotes the likes of Satan and his minions of devils and demons, but we surely don't believe Biden was referring to our fallen soldiers as demonic. At least we certainly hope not. (*Weekly Standard*, 2012).

"This is a big f---ing deal!"

More proof positive that President Barack Obama should have been keeping a bar of soap handy whenever he and Biden were anywhere near an open mic, as was the case when Biden was congratulating President Obama during the "Obamacare" health care signing ceremony, in Washington, DC (About.com, 2010).

VIDEO

"If I'm the nominee, Republicans will be sorry. The next Republican that tells me I'm not religious, I'm going to shove my rosary beads down their throat."

Not exactly the words of a compassionate Christian (*GQ*, March 2006).

"Spread your legs, you're gonna be frisked. Drop your hands to your . . . you say that to someone in North Dakota, they think it's a frisk, drop your hands to your side. They think you're in trouble, right? They tell you to drop your hands to the side. A little too formal, I know."

Notice how he keeps digging the hole deeper the more he talks. This is Biden trying to make humorous small talk during the January 2013 oath of office photo-taking session for Senator Heidi Heitkamp. Our beloved VP started in with this after the photographer requested they drop their hands. Heitkamp's husband apparently didn't find it too funny.

VIDEO

"No one making less than $250,000 under Barack Obama's plan will see one single penny of their tax raised, whether it's their capital gains tax, their income tax, investment tax, any tax."

Fun with numbers, spoken during his 2008 vice-presidential debate with Sarah Palin—as if he really believed this would hold up as true (Commission on Presidential Debates, 2008).

"Having been a receiver, I like a softer ball. That's all I can tell you."

Biden on *CBS This Morning* in January 2015 responding to a question regarding the unfolding "Deflategate" scandal in which the New England Patriots were accused of breaking rules by allegedly deflating eleven of twelve footballs in their 45-7 victory over the Indianapolis Colts in the AFC Championship game that earned the Patriots a spot in the Super Bowl (CBS News, January 21, 2015).

VIDEO

THE JOE-KER

One thing about Biden, he has a sense of humor. Whether it's a good one or a bad one is in the eye or ear of the beholder. Judge for yourself.

"I've been sleeping with a teacher for a long time. But it's always been the same teacher."

Referring to his wife Jill during a speech at a National Teacher of the Year reception (*Politico*, April 27, 2010).

"It looks like we're alone, so why don't you call me Mr. President, and I'll call you Mr. Prime Minister?"

There he goes again, Biden letting it slip in a humorous vein that the office he really covets is the one of president, not number-one jocular sidekick. Biden said this during a meeting with a British government minister, during which the UK official asked Biden how they should address each other (*The New Yorker*, July 28, 2014).

"The good news is that I can do anything I did before. The bad news is that I can't do anything better."

Speaking to about seven hundred people at the 1988 Sussex County Jamboree in Delaware, where he showed up soon after he had been released from the hospital, still in recovery mode from two brain aneurysms (*Promises to Keep*, 233).

"The single most successful, the single most persuasive, the single most strategic leader I have ever worked with is Nancy Pelosi."

The assumption here is that Biden didn't realize he was making a joke when he said this, but it sure sounds funny to many Republican loyalists. He was referring to the sometimes scatterbrained Pelosi, a Democratic US Representative from California and former Speaker of the House (*Sh*t My Vice President Says*, 42).

UNCLE JOE

When he's behaving and not saying things that make others uncomfortable, such as how he cozies up to kids with small talk at swearing-in ceremonies for senators, Biden comes across as someone you'd like to hang out with, maybe hob knob over non-alcoholic drinks with, or invite to the man cave for some serious sports viewing. He cares about people and likes people, and he likes to hear himself talk, so at least you have a friend in him who can keep the conversation going when everyone else is out of gas and looking for a smiling face to light up the room. That's Joe. He's sort of like your favorite uncle—most of the time.

"Actually, I have seen it. I wish I had your hair."

At least we know Biden is keeping up with pop culture. This is what he said when YouTube celebrity Phil DeFranco joked to Biden that he doubted that the vice president knew who he was or had ever seen his show.

VIDEO

BIDEN: "It's easy being vice president—you don't have to do anything."

INTERLOCUTOR: "It's like being the grandpa and not the parent."

BIDEN: "Yeah, that's it!"

Biden explaining his job during a casual, off-camera conversation in February 2010 that was caught by a C-SPAN mic, at a Washington, DC, health care summit (*Slate*, "The Complete Bidenisms," February 25, 2010).

"I never had an interest in being a mayor 'cause that's a real job. You have to produce. That's why I was able to be a senator for thirty-six years."

Biden speaking at a 2012 Democratic fundraiser in Chicago, while praising former Mayor Richard M. Daley (*Washington Examiner*, March 30, 2012).

"Many statements—statemen—statesmen—have walked through this campus and pronounced 'statesmen' better than I have."

Biden trying to get it right, but showing a quick recovery, during a speech at the National Defense University, Washington, DC (*Slate*, "The Complete Bidenisms," February 18, 2010).

"I'll answer your phone. I can't find mine either.
I don't know where the hell mine is."

Offering to find a ringing cell phone during a talk with seniors
at a Maryland retirement community (*Slate*, "The Complete
Bidenisms," September 23, 2009).

"Hey, guys! I'm here! You're here! We're beautiful!"

Biden making a grand entrance into Italian President Giorgio
Napolitano's palace, with his teeth gleaming and arms fully out-
stretched ready to start hugging folks (*GQ Magazine*, July 2013).

"Aw, kiddo. I feel for you. I wish I weren't the chairman; I'd come to be your lawyer."

Biden to Anita Hill, according to what she wrote in her book *Speaking Truth in Power*. During that time she was giving testimony in the Supreme Court confirmation hearings for Clarence Thomas, whom she had accused of sexual harassment from the time they worked together years earlier (*Joe Biden,* 266). Hill claims in her book that Biden said this to her during a phone call in which Hill told him she had not secured legal counsel.

"By and large I follow my own nose, and I make no apologies for being difficult to pigeonhole."

Biden's way of saying that he is a middle-of-the-road guy, perhaps skilled at 'sniffing out' problems on either side of the road (*Promises to Keep*, 105).

CRASS UNCLE JOE

Biden might be a Catholic, but he is no choir boy. When someone talks as much as he does, odds are there will always be some slippage, some junk tumbling out of his mouth that in the old days never would have made the cut on network television. Sometimes it's profanity; other times, it's just some suggestive talk and double entendres that push the envelope on what is right and proper for the vice president of the United States to be saying. Keep the bleep button close when this guy is in public and there are microphones around.

"Thanks for saving our ass."

This is what Biden stage-whispered—and what the nearby boom mics picked up—to Ford Motor Company CEO Bill Ford at an auto convention in Detroit. Biden was seated behind the wheel of an F-150 pickup truck, having just gotten a five-minute tutorial on the control panel from Ford, the only Big Three CEO not to seek a government bailout (*Politico*, March/April 2014).

"I have a f---ing target on my back."

Biden to a confidant after the 2012 budget deal (*Politico*, March/April 2014).

"As they say in my business: I'm gonna . . .
I'm gonna give you the whole load today."

Biden at a Florida rally. Not really sure where he was going with
this, but we'll keep it on the up and up and give him the benefit
of the doubt, assuming he was going to give us, as legendary
story teller Paul Harvey might have said, the rest of the story
(*Weekly Standard*).

VIDEO

"[I] fell ass over tin cup in love—at first sight."

On a spring break trip to the Bahamas during his junior year
at the University of Delaware, Biden met Neilia Hunter, a
student at Syracuse University, where he would end up going
to law school. They were married in 1966 (*New York Times*,
October 24, 2008).

"An hour late; oh give me a f---ing break."

Caught on a live mic talking to a former Senate colleague after arriving via Amtrak at Union Station in Washington, DC (Fox News, March 13, 2009).

"Did your son always have balls the size of cue balls?"

Yes, this is what Biden said to Charles Woods during a ceremony for the return of the body of Woods's son Tyrone Woods, killed in the Benghazi attacks (Blaze, 2012).

"Why don't you say something nice instead of being a smart-ass all the time?"

This is Biden speaking to a custard shop manager in June 2010 outside Milwaukee. Biden's statement above ended a brief exchange that had started as follows: "What do we owe you?" Biden is heard saying in footage captured by WISN-TV. "Don't worry, it's on us," the shop manager replied. "Lower our taxes and we'll call it even." Biden was in Wisconsin stumping for Democratic senator Russ Feingold (Fox News, October 6, 2014).

CREEPY UNCLE JOE

Sometimes it's better not to say the first thing that pops into your head. A corollary to this is if you really don't have anything constructive to say, even after you've thought it through, say nothing at all. One more thing, don't try to be cool or complimentary to kids at official state functions. Let your picture be taken with them, and shut your mouth.

"I love you, Darling."

How Biden reportedly ended his regularly scheduled telephone calls with Hillary Clinton when she was secretary of state (*HRC*, 396).

"When they're twelve to fourteen, a dad puts his beautiful little daughter to bed. And then the next morning, there's a snake in the bed."

We don't have a clue either (*Washington Post*, March 21, 2014).

"Oh man, this is boring, boring, boring. Can I borrow your hat?"

To a young boy wearing a newsboy cap in the company of Kansas Republican Pat Roberts during the January 2015 ceremonial swearing-in of senators (ABC News, 2015).

"As they say in southern Delaware,
'Boy, you married up.'"

To Maine Republican Susan Collins's husband (*National
Journal*, 2015).

"My only regret is I don't live in Wyoming."

To Wyoming Republican Michael Enzi's wife (*National Journal*,
2015).

"I've got to show you a picture of my dog, Champ."

To New Hampshire Democrat Jeanne Shaheen's family
(*National Journal*, 2015).

"Hey guys, I love your mom and your grandma."

To members of Jeanne Shaheen's family (*National Journal*, 2015).

"How old are you? Fifteen?
I hope Mom has a big fence."

To Iowa Republican Joni Ernst's teen daughter. (*National Journal*, 2015).

"See you back home, I hope."

Okay, we couldn't resist this, one more trip to a mock swearing-in ceremony and Biden's attempts to put folks and their kids at ease. Hint: It wasn't working. In this case, Biden was speaking to the young daughter of Senator Chris Coons, after he had tried to kiss her on the head while she pulled away from him. Creepy, no question (*National Journal*, 2015).

VIDEO

"You're so beautiful."

Biden to Nebraska Senator Ben Sasse's daughter (*National Journal*, 2015).

"Remember, no serious guys until you're thirty."

One of Biden's stock, if not disturbing, lines he has spoken to the daughters or granddaughters of US senators during mock swearing-in ceremonies administered by Biden (*The New Yorker*, 2014).

"You've got some eyes, Isabel, I tell you."

To an unidentified young female family member accompanying one of the senators being sworn in during a mock ceremony in January 2015 (*Western Journalism*, 2015).

VIDEO

"We have something in common: we have sisters brighter and better-looking than us."

To a woman accompanying Senator Lindsey Graham during the January 2015 mock swearing-in ceremony (*Western Journalism*, 2015).

"You have one job; keep the boys away from your sister."

Speaking to a young male family member accompanied by his sister during the January 2015 mock swearing-in ceremony (*Western Journalism*, 2015).

"You beautiful child, how are you?"

While embracing a young girl at the January 2015 mock swearing-in ceremony of senators. (*Western Journalism*, 2015)

"You've got a smile that lights up the Senate."

To an unidentified elderly woman as she walked out of the room following the January 2015 mock swearing-in ceremony for senators. (*Western Journalism*, 2015)

"Mother of ten? No purgatory for you; straight to heaven."

To a female member of Senator Dick Durbin's family. (mic. com, 2015)

"You need to work on your pecs."

Biden said this to a reporter, while tapping on his chest at a presidential campaign rally at College of Wooster in Ohio (*New York Times*, 2008).

"Those walls were awful thin. I wonder how the hell my parents did it!"

Speaking at the annual conference of a Hispanic advocacy group in Las Vegas, recalling his days growing up in a modest home (ABC News, July 10, 2012).

VIDEO

"Guess what, the cheerleaders in college are the best athletes in college. You think, I'm joking. They're almost all gymnasts; the stuff they do on hard wood, it blows my mind."

Interesting word choices while speaking at a campaign stop at Newport High School in Newport, New Hampshire. Does this guy have a clue? (*Daily Caller*, September 21, 2012)

JOE & GUNS

Despite belonging to a Democratic Party that teaches its members in Contrarianism 101 how best to hate the National Rifle Association (NRA) and overreact with outlandish condemnations of gun ownership every time there is a tragic shooting, Biden embraces firearms, and he doesn't mince words talking about it.

"So you want to keep people away in an earthquake? Buy some shotgun shells."

The vice president said this while participating in a modern-day version of a fireside chat, answering questions online about gun violence asked by four participants and a moderator on Google+. In answering one of the questions, Biden, a shotgun owner himself, said that after a deadly earthquake, a shotgun is more effective, presumably for home defense, than an assault weapon.

VIDEO

"John, every one of them, because the NRA will run a tea-bagger against you. . . . They'll put 5 million bucks against you."

Biden telling CNN's John Walsh, according to Walsh, that Republicans are scared of gun control laws because of the NRA and the Tea Party (*National Review*, July 7, 2014).

"I guarantee you: Barack Obama ain't taking my shotguns, so don't buy that malarkey. Don't buy that malarkey. They're going to start peddling that to you. I got two. If he tries to fool with my Beretta, he's got a problem."

Yeah, right. Biden at a rally in Virginia. If Obama wants to come get your guns, fella, he's going to get them. All your bluster ain't going to stop him or the US Attorney General, or whoever comes to collect them.

VIDEO

"Just fire the shotgun through the door."

This was Biden's strange advice given to *Field and Stream*, aimed at those looking to protect themselves against would-be intruders (Blaze, April 12, 2013).

"If you want to protect yourself, get a double-barrel shotgun. . . . You don't need an AR-15. It's harder to aim. It's harder to use. And in fact, you don't need thirty rounds to protect yourself. Buy a shotgun. Buy a shotgun."

From a February 2013 video interview with *Parents Magazine* about reducing gun violence (parents.com February 19, 2013). The article went on to quote Texas gun shop owner Jesse Bonner pointing out inaccuracies in Biden's statement: "That would not be true," Bonner said. "I've taught enough ladies to shoot all different types of firearms, and I can tell you that the AR-15 is going to be better suited for a lady. It would be better for all-around home defense, and it's one of the most accurate guns out there. The AR-15 is now a mainstream weapon because of its quality design and accuracy."

VIDEO

"Kinda scary man, the black helicopter crowd is really upset. No way that Uncle Sam can go find out whether you own a gun because we're about to really take away all your rights and you're not going to be able to defend yourself and we're going to swoop down with Special Forces folks and gather up every gun in America. It's bizarre. But that's what's being sold out there."

Many gun owners envision such a scenario described here by Biden, and they don't see it as a bizarre view of the world at all. In saying this, Biden was touting proposed gun control measures and criticizing the NRA. This was his way of mocking gun owners concerned over potential government overreach in regulating firearms (Blaze, April 12, 2013).

"Use a shotgun . . . and you don't kill your kids."

Biden was saying to stay away from AR-15s, which, he said, could kill American children (Blaze, April 12, 2013).

JOE THE POLITICIAN

Joe Biden is the poster boy for career politicians, having sought and served in public office since his mid-twenties. One thing he knows very well is politics and all its nuances and hidden secrets, and he has never been shy about showing his expertise on the subject, whether it be wittingly or unwittingly.

"In this world, emotion has become suspect—the accepted style is smooth, antiseptic, and passionless."

Anyone who has listened to Biden enough times while he's speaking in public might argue he is none of those three things (*New York Times*, June 10, 1987). He said this in 1987 during his first run for the presidency.

"'Obama and Biden want to raise taxes by a trillion dollars.' Guess what? Yes, we do in one regard: We want to let that trillion-dollar tax cut expire so the middle class doesn't have to bear the burden of all that money going to the super-wealthy. That's not a tax raise. That's called fairness where I come from."

That's called BS where the rest of us come from. Spoken during the 2012 presidential campaign. (*Weekly Standard*, October 4, 2012).

"Chris is getting the living hell beat out of him, the living bejesus beat out of him."

Biden telling it like it is, and no one would argue with what he was saying, in assessing Democratic Senator Chris Dodd's sagging poll numbers during a 2009 fundraiser for the Connecticut senator (*Slate*, spoken December 11, 2009).

"We're going to control the insurance companies. You know people aren't going to lose their health care with their employer like is being advertised."

Biden, much like his boss, Obama, regaling us with the alleged benefits of Obamacare. It would be amusing if it weren't such, as he might say, a load of malarkey (ABC News, 2010).

"Ladies and gentlemen, folks, this is not a country of victims. . . . And so when I hear Romney and Ryan and this new Republican Party in Congress talk about the climb in dependency, I give you my word, I don't know what country they're living in."

What planet are you from, Mr. Vice President? This is a classic example of a shameless Democrat stealing phrases usually spoken with sincerity by Republicans and making it his or her own. This is Biden mimicking the likes of Ronald Reagan and turning an opposing but popular viewpoint into his own. And, yes, Joe, there has been a climb in government-enabled dependency in recent years. This old political con of deny, deny, deny just doesn't cut it (*Politico*, September 21, 2012).

"Good luck following that."

Biden to Hillary Clinton as she stood up to give the eulogy at late senator Frank Lautenberg's funeral service in June 2013 immediately after Broadway star Brian Stokes Mitchell had sung an incredible song (*HRC*, 396).

"Ultimately, as long as Saddam Hussein is at the helm, no inspectors can guarantee that they have rooted out the entirety of Saddam Hussein's weapons program. The only way to remove Saddam is a massive military effort, led by the United States."

Biden, writing in the *Washington Post*, after Saddam Hussein in 1998 insisted that international weapons inspectors stop work and leave Iraq. Congress subsequently passed and President Clinton signed into law the Iraq Liberation Act, making regime change in Iraq the policy of the United States government and opening the door to military action. Make no mistake about it; there was strong bipartisan support for military action against Iraq long before 9/11 and Biden was a big part of that (*In My Time*, 366).

"If we wait for the danger to become clear, it could be too late."

Biden, in 2002, about six months before the United States finally invaded Iraq following the terrorist attacks of 9/11 (ontheissues.org). This is presented here just to remind folks that long before Democrats, such as Biden, started getting all weaselly and backtracking on all this for the political expediency of being able to say that a Republican presidential administration had gotten us into an ill-conceived (debatable) military action, there was strong bipartisan support for such action. Hindsight has made geniuses out of many liberals, in their minds (Doonesbury.com's *The War in Quotes*, 29).

"Vice President Cheney has been the most dangerous vice president we've had probably in American history."

Stated during his 2008 vice-presidential debate with Sarah Palin. Some could say Biden inherited that title, if for nothing else than the risk he takes every time he opens his mouth (*Politico*, December 6, 2008).

"There are things that have occurred in this campaign, in every campaign, that I'm sure both of us regret . . . particularly in these special new groups that can go out there, raise all the money they want, not have to identify themselves, and say the most scurrilous things about the other candidate. It's an abomination."

Biden assessing the 2012 presidential race, in which Obama and he were seeking re-election against the Republican ticket of Mitt Romney and Paul Ryan (*Politico*, October 11, 2012).

"And don't any of you, by the way, any of you guys vote Republican. I'm not supposed to say, this isn't political . . . don't come to me if you do! You're on your own, Jack!"

Biden telling Teamsters union members in Las Vegas to be careful with their 2012 vote while addressing them during their annual convention (Fox News, 2012).

"I am absolutely comfortable with the fact that men marrying men, women marrying women, and heterosexual men and women marrying another are entitled to the same exact rights, all the civil rights, all the civil liberties. And quite frankly, I don't see much of a distinction beyond that."

Biden on *Meet the Press* in May 2012 (ABC News, May 6, 2012). One problem with this: Biden's boss, President Obama, had not yet come out publicly in support of gay marriage, and Biden was beating him to the punch. Not smart.

VIDEO

"Gird your loins."

Biden in Seattle, perhaps borrowing from a *Smokey and the Bandit* script, speaking at a fundraiser two weeks out from the 2008 presidential election about how much of a task it would be to repair the economy (*Slate*, October 20, 2008).

"This is deadly earnest, man. This is deadly earnest. How can they justify . . . how can they justify raising taxes on the middle class that has been buried the last four years? How in Lord's name can they justify raising their taxes with these tax cuts?"

In saying this at a campaign rally, Biden failed to remind the folks that those last four years he was talking about? Those were four years under President Obama and Biden (Fox News, October 2, 2012). At least Biden was right: he was being earnest.

VIDEO

"Mitt Romney, Rick Santorum, and Newt Gingrich, these guys have a fundamentally different economic philosophy than we do. . . . Simply stated, we're about promoting the private sector, they're about protecting the privileged sector."

Biden speaking at a political rally in Toledo, Ohio, offering more hypocritical pabulum about the so-called privileged sector of our society, which liberals will have you believe is made up of about 99.9 percent Republicans. Note, though, the timing of Biden's message here: Just two days earlier, his boss, President Obama, and visiting British prime minister David Cameron, had gone joyriding in Air Force One, zipping over to an NCAA Tournament men's basketball game in nearby Dayton, Ohio (*Daily Caller*, March 15, 2012). Keep in mind, at the time, the cost of operating Air Force One was about $180,000 per hour. So, who's privileged now?

VIDEO

"Find enough beautiful women and enough guys will show up. . . . *The Hill* newspaper is here, and they'll think that's a sexist remark."

Oh, you mean to say it is not a sexist remark? This is Biden explaining, to some young supporters in Washington, DC, one of his secrets to successful fundraising (*Slate*, October 31, 2005).

"They sound like squealing pigs."

Biden speaking in Minnesota about Republicans. He was referencing, as he described it, how Republicans were opposing Democratic plans to toughen regulations on Wall Street (ABC News, August 21, 2012).

"With all due respect, you've told me nothing. It's kind of interesting, this kabuki dance we have in these hearings here, as if the public doesn't have a right to know what you think about fundamental issues facing them. Without any knowledge of your understanding of the law, because you will not share it with us, we are rolling the dice with you, Judge."

Biden to Supreme Court nominee John Roberts in 2005, during the confirmation hearings for Roberts. Biden said this after Roberts had explained his views on privacy and his legal philosophy (CNN, September 14, 2005).

"Wait, there's Little Italy down there. A lot of great Italian restaurants. If there's anybody down there who doesn't vote for me, I haven't found them yet. But I will. I will."

Biden looking out the window of an SUV while taking a tour through his old stomping grounds in Wilmington, Delaware, accompanied by a magazine reporter (*GQ Magazine*, July 2013).

"I can die a happy man never having been president of the United States of America. But it doesn't mean I won't run"

Biden telling *GQ Magazine* in a July 2013 profile on him that, at the time, he hadn't ruled out running for president in 2016. As this book went to press in July 2015, he hadn't yet publicly announced his plans for 2016.

"And by the way, if you come in the office, I have two portraits hanging—one of Jefferson, one of Adams. Both vice presidents who became presidents. I joke to myself, 'I wonder what their portraits looked like when they were vice presidents.'"

(*GQ Magazine*, July 2013)

"And I said, 'Why do you want me to be vice president?' He said, 'Help me govern. Joe, you do Iraq, defense, state—talk to Joe. Get it done. Recovery Act, almost a trillion dollars, do it, Joe!' Not that I'm so special, or that he couldn't do it as well or better. But guess what, there was a war in Afghanistan going on at the same time, a banking system collapsing. It was a boulder rolling down a hill here."

Biden reliving a conversation he had with Barack Obama in which Obama explained to Biden what his role as vice president would be (*GQ Magazine*, July 2013).

"The only thing I know is I ain't changing my brand. I know what I believe. I'm confident in what I know. And I'm gonna say it. And if folks like it, wonderful. If they don't like it, I understand."

(*Politico*, March/April 2014)

"This is not your father's Republican Party. This is a different breed of cat, man. I am not making a moral judgment, but I will tell you that they have no judgment."

More of his rantings against the Republican Party, when he could say the same thing about his own party (CNN, October 14, 2014).

"I'm not used to these standing ovations; I'm a vice president."

Speaking at the 21st Annual National Fire and Emergency Services Dinner in Washington, DC, in 2009 (*Los Angeles Times*, 2009).

"Has anyone ever blamed a man for being drunk?"

Biden sometimes makes a good point, but just has a funny way of saying it. Here he is addressing the double standards of a culture that often blames the woman for "putting herself in a position" to be victimized (dailytexanonline.com, March 28, 2014).

"You know, eleven million people living in the shadows; I believe they're already American citizens. . . . These people are just waiting, waiting for a chance to be able to contribute fully. And by that standard, eleven million undocumented persons are already Americans, in my view."

Political correctness at its finest: Biden not only saying that it's okay for illegal immigrants to be in the United States, but, hey, while we're at it, let's just go ahead and make them American citizens. Just do it. Chalk up a few more million votes on election day for those kind-hearted Democrats (glennbeck.com, March 28, 2014).

"After the worst job loss since the Great Depression, we've created 4.5 million private sector jobs in the past twenty-nine months."

It is assumed Biden said this with a straight face, speaking at the 2012 Democratic National Convention, although he definitely used some fuzzy math. What Biden's statement fails to mention is that it doesn't account for jobs lost during Obama's time in office up to that point or the fact that joblessness had risen overall in his first term (*National Journal*, September 6, 2012; from the transcript of Biden's speech).

"Look, I just have more of a populist strain than Barack does."

He reportedly said this to an associate, perhaps looking to distance himself from Obama and be his own man in preparation for a 2016 run for the presidency (*Politico*, March/April 2014).

"All politics is personal. In the neighborhood where I come from, where these folks come from, everybody knows they've got to chip in. What they don't like is turning around and finding they are being played for a sucker."

(Newsfeed.time.com, August 10, 2012)

"I had the sensation of speech, but I'm not sure I knew what I was saying; I had the feeling of being outside my own body, watching. I have no memory of finishing the speech, no memory of leaving the floor."

Biden recalling his maiden speech on the Senate floor soon after taking office in January 1972. This description would help explain some of the many other things he has spoken in public over the years (*Promises to Keep*, 91).

"I think I instinctively understood that my most important duty was to be a target. People were desperate to vent their anger, and if they could yell at a United States senator, all the better."

(*Promises to Keep*, 127)

"'Look,' I told them, 'I was against busing to remedy de facto segregation owing to housing patterns and community comfort, but if it was intentional segregation, I'd personally pay for helicopters to move the children.' There were howls in the crowd. I stand by the statement, but it was probably the single stupidest moment I could have chosen to make it."

Biden recalling the time he spoke to several hundred citizens packed into a school gymnasium near Wilmington. The touchy subject was busing, and Biden was on the wrong side of the issue for a Democrat (*Promises to Keep,* 128).

"You thump that Bible one more time,
and you're going to lose me too."

As a young senator to Jimmy Carter during one of Carter's
presidential campaigns (*Promises to Keep*, 135).

"He just sat like a bullfrog on a log, listening."

Biden describing his predecessor Vice President Dick Cheney's
demeanor during meetings with President George W. Bush
(*Promises to Keep*, 336).

"I've reached my ultimate goal!"

Biden upon winning his 1972 US Senate race in Delaware,
although we've long known he wasn't being truthful even then
(*Joe Biden*, 90).

"I give you my word as a Biden."

Reportedly, one of Biden's pet sayings when making a point he
vows to be true, but who's to say how much stock to put into
that declaration (*Joe Biden*, 195).

"I am no less frustrated at the environment of presidential politics that makes it so difficult to let the American people measure the whole Joe Biden and not just misstatements that I have made."

From Biden's statement announcing his withdrawal from the 1988 presidential race. One of those misstatements happened to be his, no pun intended, liberal use of segments of a speech from British Labor Party leader Neil Kinnock in his own campaign speech in 1987, without attributing Kinnock. Biden said it was an honest mistake, while critics called it plagiarism. In all fairness to Biden, he had referenced the Kinnock speech in previous speeches of his, although in those cases he had been careful to give attribution to Kinnock (*Joe Biden,* 215).

"I knew I had to be sure-footed about the issues I was talking about. When you're twenty-nine years old, who the hell is going to think you're credible? It wasn't enough to have ideas; I had to know my facts. I had to demonstrate command from the minute I started running. I understood that was the test I had to pass."

Biden was twenty-nine when in 1972 he won one of Delaware's two US Senate seats, turning thirty (the minimum age to be a US senator) between Election Day and when he was sworn in to office in January 1973 (*Promises to Keep*, 63).

"I mean if I run, I'm confident I will be able to mount a campaign that (is) . . . gonna be credible. And I'm gonna be serious."

Well, the part about his pledge to be serious was a good sign, even if voters aren't serious about him (*Politico*, March/April 2014).

"My issues were voting rights, civil rights, crime, clean water and clean air, pension protection, health care, and the war in Vietnam. That day in 1972 I called for a comprehensive national health care program."

Biden pretty much checking off all the boxes in the liberal politician's playbook during his first run for the US Senate, in 1972 (*Joe Biden*, 73).

"I was the Barack Obama!"

Biden in 2008 recalling to a reporter his presidential run of twenty years earlier, when he had concentrated so much on selling his passion for change that he neglected to bring the substance of his campaign platform to the table (*Joe Biden*, 387).

"I am running for president. I'm going to be Joe Biden, and I'm going to try to be the best Biden I can be. If I can, I've got a shot. If I can't, I lose."

Announcing his entry for the 2008 presidential race on January 7, 2007, on NBC's *Meet the Press*. We can only assume he was not the best Biden he could be during his short-lived campaign, pulling a miniscule percentage of the vote in the Iowa caucuses and dropping out of the Democratic primary race soon after (*Joe Biden*, 372).

"I really, genuinely know what I believe and what I would do as president. I have a comfort zone. There's not any nobility about it; it's just that I'm okay."

Addressing how he perceived his fitness for the presidency in 2008 (*Joe Biden*, 388).

CLUELESS JOE

Throughout much of his political career, and we would dare say predating even that time, Biden has demonstrated himself to be clueless, either by deed or more often by word. For the sake of this book, we'll focus on the latter part for now.

"I happened to be literally—probably, it turned out, to be a quarter of a mile [away] at an outing when I heard gunshots in the woods. We didn't know . . . we thought they were hunters."

In January 2013 at a meeting of mayors in Washington, DC, Biden claimed he heard gunshots from the 2006 Amish school shooting in Pennsylvania while allegedly playing golf nearby. The *Washington Times* checked it out and not only failed to find a golf course in the vicinity of where the shooting took place, but could find no record of Biden even playing golf anywhere in that vicinity on that day (*Washington Times*, January 18, 2013).

"I've been doing this for a long time. Not as long as my friend Dennis Ross, who's with me—Roth, who's with me—Ross, who's with me. . . . He's with me."

Speaking at Tel Aviv University in Israel, March 11, 2010. Ross . . . Roth . . . Ross . . . oh, what the heck. We're with you on this one, Joe (*Slate* April 30, 2010).

"Cleveland Plain Dealer, one of the major newspapers in this state, said, 'It's a masterpiece in misdirection.'"

One big problem with this one: Cleveland is in Ohio, and at the time Biden said this he was campaigning in Florida. Talk about misdirection (*Cleveland Plain Dealer*, November 2, 2012).

VIDEO

"Look, the Taliban per se is not our enemy. That's critical. There is not a single statement that the president has ever made in any of our policy assertions that the Taliban is our enemy because it threatens US interests. If, in fact, the Taliban is able to collapse the existing government, which is cooperating with us in keeping the bad guys from being able to do damage to us, then that becomes a problem for us."

The Taliban not our enemy? Be serious. (*Newsweek*, December 19, 2011).

"I got tested for AIDS. I know Barack got tested for AIDS. There's no shame in being tested for AIDS. It's an important thing."

Well, this is good to know. Biden said this at the third Democratic Primary Presidential Debate at Howard University in June 2007. (*New York Times*, June 28, 2007).

"I mean it, literally, ladies and gentleman, this is a guy who's running all the ads here in Iowa, saying he's gonna get tough on China. I've been in ... I've had the great privilege of being able to be in this state now. I think it's my twenty-fifth event; I'm not sure. But I've been all over the state."

Once again, geography alert! Biden this time was speaking in Ohio, not in Iowa as he states here during the 2012 presidential race (Fox News, October 24, 2012).

VIDEO

"Look, all you have to do is go down Union Street with me in Wilmington or go to Katie's Restaurant or walk into Home Depot with me where I spend a lot of time, and you ask anybody in there whether or not the economic and foreign policy of this administration has made them better off in the last eight years."

Spoken during his VP candidates' debate with Sarah Palin in 2008. Well, truth be told, they were not better off at Katie's Restaurant. It had been shuttered since the Clinton years (*National Review*, October 4, 2008).

"I may be Irish, but I'm not stupid."

Spoken to South Carolina senator Lindsey Graham during the ceremonial swearing-in for senators in January 2015, although we believe Biden was joking (NBC News, January 6, 2015).

"If you want to know where Al Qaeda lives—you want to know where Bin Laden is, come back to Afghanistan with me. Come back to the area where my helicopter was forced down, with a three-star general and three senators at ten thousand five hundred feet in the middle of those mountains. I can tell you where they are."

Another of Biden's Brian Williams-like moments—remembering things as he wished them to be versus what actually took place. He said this while addressing National Guard members in Baltimore in September 2008, failing to point out the whole story: that the landing had been forced because of a sudden snowstorm and not because of any enemy action as this statement might imply (Associated Press, October 2, 2008).

"Come on up here, Frank . . . Bob."

Biden calling up New Jersey senator Bob Menendez to join him at the podium for the swearing-in of new New Jersey senator Cory Booker, who was taking the place of Frank Lautenburg, who had died earlier that year (2013) at the age of eighty-nine (*Huffington Post*, November 8, 2013).

"You son of a gun, Marty! You did it!"

Biden congratulating Marty Walsh over the telephone for winning the Boston mayoral race in 2013. A great moment for Marty, right? Not exactly. It was the wrong Marty Walsh. Biden had called the Marty Walsh who's a former aide to Senator Ted Kennedy and at the time the president of a Boston government relations firm. The "right" Marty Walsh was a labor activist and state lawmaker who'd just won the top city hall job. (*Christian Science Monitor*, November 7, 2013).

"I don't own a single stock or bond. I have no savings account."

Ehhh, that's not exactly true. Biden's attempt to paint himself as a working-class politician while speaking at a White House summit on working families didn't exactly pan out. He conveniently omitted the fact that he has hundreds of thousands of dollars in stocks, bonds, and savings in his wife Jill's name (*Washington Post*, June 23, 2014).

"Neither he and I are technology geeks and we assumed that it was up and ready to run."

Biden referring to Obama and himself in explaining the failure of the Obamacare website to be ready to launch at the appointed time. And for you grammarians, that "he and I" reference is indeed what came out of his mouth.

VIDEO

"I don't know. I wish I could tell you. That's why I became a lawyer."

When asked why it was taking so long to fix the mess known as the Obamacare website (*National Review*, October 31, 2013).

VIDEO

"I'm proud of you."

Telling the park ranger at the World War II Memorial in Washington, DC, that he was proud of the ranger's actions in standing up to and keeping out some folks trying to get a better look at the shuttered tourist site. Perhaps Biden was not aware that the people being denied access were some World War II veterans as well as Republican congressman Randy Neugebauer (*Washington Examiner*, October 4, 2013).

"I'm going to say something outrageous. I think I understand the Senate better than any man or woman who's ever served in there."

Spoken while taking credit for the Violence against Women Act. And he was right about one thing—it was an outrageous statement (*Weekly Standard*, September 13, 2013).

"But I always say what I mean."

Highly debatable. Biden's retort to Paul Ryan during the 2012 vice presidential debate when Ryan took Biden to task for his penchant for often not getting things quite right when speaking in public. Ryan said to Biden, "I think the vice president very well knows, that sometimes the words don't come out of your mouth the right away" (*New York Daily News*, October 12, 2012).

VIDEO

"We have turned this economy around. Instead of falling off the abyss, it is on firm ground. It is heading in the right direction. And every aspect of the economy is growing."

At times like this Biden comes across as a used-car salesman, which isn't that far-fetched. After all, his dad, Joe Sr., did sell cars (whitehouse.gov, June 17, 2010).

"Well, we weren't told they wanted more security there. We did not know they wanted more security again. And by the way, at the time we were told exactly—we said exactly what the intelligence community told us that they knew. That was the assessment. And as the intelligence community changed their view, we made it clear they changed their view."

A classic political deflection. This was Biden's attempt to sidestep responsibility on the part of the presidential administration regarding the October 2012 terrorists attack on the American embassy in Benghazi, Libya, that took the lives of four Americans (*Tampa Bay Times*, October 18, 2012).

"As I said just before the President signed the health care bill, I quoted Virgil, the classic Greek poet, who once said, 'The greatest wealth is health.' The greatest wealth is health. Mr. President, you've made us a nobler and wealthier nation by providing for the health of your fellow citizens."

Wow, such a noble-sounding statement from a regular Joe. Give this guy a stone tablet and the means to etch this message, and we can save it for all of posterity. One problem, though. Virgil was not Greek; he was Roman. He was even buried in Naples. Then again, maybe this whole deal about being the number-two guy in America is all Greek to Biden. One other thing – some scholars have questioned if Virgil even wrote this (whitehouse .gov, March 23, 2010).

"Folks, where's it written we cannot lead the world in the twentieth century in making automobiles?"

Better yet, now that we've left Y2K way behind in the rear-view mirror, let's focus on leading the world in cars made for the twenty-first century, our current time. Wrong century, Joe (*Weekly Standard,* August 15, 2012).

"Better than everybody else. You don't know my state. My state was a slave state. My state is a border state. My state is the eighth largest black population in the country. My state is anything from a northeast liberal state."

Biden's answer, during an interview on *Fox News Sunday,* in the lead-up to the 2008 presidential race, to a question about how he, as a "northeast liberal," could compete against more conservative southern candidates. Keep in mind that Biden's state is Delaware, north of Maryland, tucked in between New Jersey and Pennsylvania. This statement is more proof that a politician will say just about anything in an attempt to con enough affected voters into believing him (CNN, February 9, 2007).

"[Delaware is a] slave state that fought beside the North. That's only because we couldn't figure out how to get to the South. There were a couple of states in the way."

Biden said this when speaking to the Columbia Rotary Club in South Carolina in December 2006, according to a story published in *The State* newspaper (CNN, February 9, 2007).

"At the time I had no intention of serving more than six months."

Biden in his memoir, *Promises to Keep*, recalling what his thinking was when he was first elected to the U.S. Senate, in 1972. Maybe he just didn't realize his term was for six years, not six months (*Promises to Keep*, xviii).

NO ORDINARY ORATOR

Biden is not someone you would call a great orator; he occasionally messes things up. But he is a good public speaker who smiles a lot and brings a lot of energy to the table or to the mic. Whereas his boss, President Obama, relies heavily on a teleprompter in speeches, Biden is the king of winging it. He can be entertaining, even when not trying, and his willingness to speak off the cuff, while it does get him in trouble at times, is more refreshing than listening to Obama carefully choosing his closely guarded words.

"I think this is pretty important to understand. I really mean this. Maybe it's just me. Maybe he makes me so . . . So I'm being a good Biden today."

Biden apparently lost in thought, catching himself before saying something he knows he will regret. This is the equivalent of the golfer who is able to stop his swing in his backswing when distracted by a loud noise or an unruly spectator. Easier said than done.

VIDEO

"Stop moving that . . . that . . . that . . . that . . . that . . . uh, you know, what's this thing called? You know, a teleprompter. Barack always kids when he says, 'Joe Biden,' he said, 'I'm learning to speak without a teleprompter; Joe's learning to speak with one.'"

(*Weekly Standard*, March 21, 2014)

"Look what I learned is I'm not changing my brand. There's nothing I've said that I haven't said that was truthful. And so sometimes – you know, everybody says they're looking for authenticity."

That explains a lot (CNN, November 3, 2014).

"Thank you, Dr. Pepper, and thank you, Chancell . . .
Dr. Paper, and thank you, Chancellor."

This was at a campaign stop in Iowa in March 2012, Biden accidentally thanked "Dr. Pepper" for helping to organize the event, although he meant Scott Community College president Dr. Theresa Paper. But he quickly caught his mistake and corrected himself.

VIDEO

"Make sure of two things. Be careful—microphones are always hot, and understand that in Washington, DC, a gaffe is when you tell the truth. So, be careful."

Sound advice given during a speech at a Washington, DC, national conference of the National Association of Black Journalists (*Politico*, June 20, 2012).

"I said, 'I sit back there and I listen. I helped write the ideas in the speech—I know it all. But I've got to pay attention.' And she said, 'Welcome to the good wives club— how many times have I sat there and listened to you make a speech and pretended to be interested?'"

Biden to talk show host Ellen DeGeneres, talking about President Obama's State of the Union addresses and relating a conversation he had with his wife, Jill (*Washington Post*, January 26, 2015).

"I exaggerate when I'm angry, but I've never gone around telling people things that aren't true about me."

Biden referring to the time in New Hampshire in 1987 during his first run for the presidency when he claimed to have a higher IQ than someone who had questioned him about his academic performance in college. (*New York Times*, September 21, 1987).

"I guess every single word I've ever said is going to be dissected now."

Biden acknowledging that his past misstatements about his level of success (or lack thereof) in college were now catching up to him during his first try at the presidency (*New York Times*, September 21, 1987).

"Every ridiculous assertion from Dr. Carson on— I mean Jesus, God. Oh God. I mean, it's kind of hard to fathom, isn't it?"

A coming-to-Jesus moment for Biden? Not hardly, although that's probably about as reverent as Biden will ever get in public—although he wasn't exactly being prayerful here in his mentions of deity. In fact, he was taking to task Dr. Ben Carson, a prominent neurosurgeon and Republican candidate for the presidency in 2016, for comments attributed to Carson in March 2015. Carson made comments indicating that he believed homosexuality is a choice, comments Carson later said he regretted making (MSNBC, March 6, 2015).

PI JOE

The PI stands for Politically Incorrect. It's a label that fits Biden, at times. Although Biden is a lifelong Democrat, and a somewhat liberal one at that, every now and then he slips up and makes a case for being a bit conservative in his heart.

"I told the President, next game I have him (Kevin Johnson). Just remember, I may be a white boy, but I can jump."

Spoken at an event honoring African-American history month, where Biden was joined by former NBA star Kevin Johnson, now Sacramento's mayor (*Political Ticker*, CNN blog, February 25, 2014).

VIDEO

"My mother has an expression: clean as a whistle, sharp as a tack."

As for his use of the word *clean* here and in other places, Biden said he was referring to a phrase used by his mother (CNN, January 31, 2007).

"The Turks . . . the Saudis, the Emiratis, etc. What were they doing? They were so determined to take down [Syrian President Bashar] Assad and essentially have a proxy Sunni-Shia war."

Biden speaking in 2014 at Harvard University. He touched off a diplomatic snafu by suggesting that some of our allies in the fight against Islamic State (ISIS) were giving money and arms to extremists, which we now believe not to have been the case (Fox News, October 6, 2014).

"Barack Obama is probably the most exciting candidate that the Democratic or Republican Party has produced, at least since I've been around. And he's fresh. He's new. He's smart. He's insightful. And I really regret that some have taken totally out of context my use of the world 'clean.'"

Biden digging that hole a bit deeper in terms of his attempt to compliment his future boss with more questionable use of adjectives. At this point he probably would have been better zipping it on that subject, once and for all (CNN, January 31, 2007).

"I deeply regret any offense my remark in the *New York Observer* might have caused anyone. That was not my intent and I expressed that to Senator Obama."

Biden apologizing for calling Obama "the first mainstream African-American who is articulate and bright and clean and a nice-looking guy" (CNN, January 31, 2007).

"I have some friends on the far Left, and they can justify to me the murder of a white deaf mute for a nickel by five colored guys. But they can't justify some Alabama farmers tar-and-feathering an old colored woman. I suspect the ACLU would leap to defend the five black guys. But no one would go to help the 'rednecks.'"

(*Joe Biden*, 60–61)

"I think that the only reason Clarence Thomas is on the [Supreme] Court is because he is black. I don't believe he could have won had he been white."

(*Joe Biden*, 283)

"There's a big difference in this race. Barack Obama's not at the head of the ticket. And that means those legions of African Americans and Latinos are not automatically going to come out. No one has energized them like Barack Obama. But he's not on the ticket. So don't take this one for granted."

Biden said this concerning the Massachusetts Senate special election of 2013 with Biden, in essence, admitting that race is a factor that works both sides of an election (*Washington Post*, June 11, 2013).

JOE THE DUMBER

During the 2008 presidential campaign season, Republican presidential candidate John McCain and the GOP had an ordinary joe on their side we called "Joe the Plumber," who proved himself a worthy thorn in the side of Barack Obama's Democratic campaign for president. That gave the Republicans Joe the Plumber; meanwhile, Democrats have been stuck with "Joe the Dumber" going on forty-five years now. That's not to say that Joe Biden is a dumb guy. He's really not, although, he will never be accused of being shrewd or particularly savvy. Let's just come right out and say it: sometimes Biden can say and do some really dumb things.

"Hey, Bonita, I'm Joe. Not the plumber;
Joe the Biden."

Greeting a woman during a presidential election campaign stop
in Ocala, Florida, in October 2008 (*Slate*, April 30, 2010).

"Am I doing this again? For the senior staff? My
memory is not as good as Chief Justice Roberts's."

Mocking Supreme Court Chief Justice John Roberts's briefly
botched effort to swear in Barack Obama for his first presidential term. Biden was set to swear in White House senior staff one
day after the Inauguration snafu, in Washington, DC, January
2009 (*Time*, January 21, 2009).

"Jill and I had the great honor of standing on that stage, looking across at one of the great justices, Justice Stewart."

Mistakenly referring to Justice John Paul Stevens, who swore Biden in as vice president in January 2009 (Fox News, October 6, 2014).

VIDEO

"When my first semester grades came out, my mom and dad told me I wouldn't be playing football."

(*Promises to Keep*, 26)

"There are more rigs, gas and oil rigs, in the United States pumping today than every other nation in the world combined. Combined. North America will account, meaning Mexico, China, and Canada, for two-thirds of the growth of global energy supply over the next twenty years."

During a speech at Harvard, perhaps forgetting or just ignorant to the fact that China is not part of North America (CNS News, October 3, 2014).

"There's no reason the nation of Africa cannot and should not join the ranks of the world's most prosperous nations in the near term, in the decades ahead."

Speaking at a US/Africa summit (*Washington Free Beacon*, August 5, 2014). More issues with world geography: Africa is not a country; it's a continent.

"My God, you have survived and you have soared. It was worth—it was worth it. I mean it sincerely."

Speaking to victims of the 2013 Boston Marathon bombings on the first anniversary of the tragedy, in which several people were killed and hundreds of others severely injured, many having limbs blown off from the blasts. I doubt most, if not all, of the victims have ever thought it was "worth it." (*The Wire*, April 15, 2014).

VIDEO

"I spent half my life on our national security council."

Do the math—this would make Biden about eight years old at the time he said this (*Weekly Standard*, February 5, 2013).

"But you can't erase what you've already done. They voted to extend tax cuts for the very wealthy, giving a $500 trillion tax cut to 120,000 families."

This is Biden's way of going one up on President Obama, whose own amazing claim had been for a $5 trillion tax cut. Truly amazing . . . and implausible (*Washington Examiner*, October 26, 2012).

VIDEO

"They have acted like terrorists."

While Obama and Biden have for years danced around using the word *terrorists* to describe members of violent organizations, such as the Islamic State (ISIS) and al-Qaeda, Biden didn't hesitate to use the word to criticize Republicans—US Republicans, no less—for how they negotiated the federal debt limit (*Politico*, August 1, 2011).

"Somalis, who have made my city of Wilmington, Delaware, [their home] . . . I have great relationships with them because there's an awful lot of them driving cabs and are friends of mine. For real. I'm not being solicitous. I'm being serious."

Biden speaking at a roundtable discussion on violent extremism, insisting how popular he is with the Somali community in his hometown of Wilmington, Delaware. He brought this up as an analogy to what is going on in Minneapolis-St. Paul, Minnesota, regarding East African immigrants moving there. Being friends with Somalis is not dumb, but how Biden goes about saying stuff like this is just, well, let's just say if a Republican were to say something culturally stereotypical like this, they would be figuratively mauled by the mainstream media. But Biden gets a free pass on dumb stuff like this because it is expected of him (*Washington Post*, February 17, 2015).

VIDEO

"When he [Biden's son, Beau] was over there in Iraq for a year, people would come to him and talk about what was happening to them at home in terms of foreclosures, in terms of bad loans that were being . . . I mean these Shylocks who took advantage of these women and men while overseas."

The vice president stepped in the stuff again while speaking to the Legal Services Corporation by using the expression "shylocks," which is generally regarded as a derogatory term referring to people of the Jewish faith (CNN, September 17, 2014).

VIDEO

"They're hard on me, man. This vice president stuff is tough."

Aw, quit complaining. We've already heard stuff like this from you before. Suck it up, Joe. Stated while making a campaign stop at a Hy-Vee Store in Iowa (*Breitbart*, October 4, 2012).

"The economy is getting worse for a number of reasons. Let me be precise. It's not that it's getting worse. It's not getting better at the rate it should get better."

That's one way of looking at it . . . in Spin City, maybe (*The Atlantic*, October 6, 2011). He said this during an interview with David Gregory at the Newseum in Washington, DC.

VIDEO

"[Y]ou have on the one end Van Jones's guys, whoever he is."

Biden speaking on a Florida radio show referring to a guy he should know well—he supposedly had vetted Jones for the position of Green Czar in the Obama White House (*Huffington Post*, October 4, 2011).

"You all were here before us. The contributions being made to this country by Hispanic Americans is well over four hundred years old."

Another math problem—America has been a country only about 240 years. Biden said this while hosting the annual Hispanic Heritage Month reception at the Naval Observatory (*Politico*, September 30, 2011).

"I think I probably have a much higher IQ than you do, I suspect. I went to law school on a full academic scholarship--the only one in my class to have a full academic scholarship. . . . I won the international moot court competition. I was the outstanding student in the political science department at the end of my year. I graduated with three degrees from undergraduate school, and 165 credits—only needed 123—and I'd be delighted to sit down and compare my IQ to yours."

This is actually a Biden tirade from his brief 1988 presidential campaign. It's his response when asked by a prospective voter where he went to law school (Syracuse University) and apparently that question struck a nerve with Biden, perhaps in part because he had graduated seventy-sixth in a class of eighty-five. (*Weekly Standard*, December 21, 2009).

VIDEO

"[R]emember your college days, having to study the essayist Samuel Johnson? And one of the favorite quotes I remember, Mr. Secretary, was 'There is nothing like a hanging to focus one's attention.'"

It's one thing to be able to quote literature as Biden obviously does here, presumably aiming to demonstrate his intellectual credibility, but certainly there's a better choice of words when talking to a benign jobs summit (*Weekly Standard*, December 21, 2009).

"You've got a really tough job. If the Lord Almighty came down and gave us 60 percent of the right answers, we'd still have a less-than-even chance of making this work."

Biden in 2003 discussing the mess in post-war Iraq with Paul Bremer, the appointed civilian head of the Coalition Provisional Authority, which was tasked with the reconstruction of Iraq (*Promises to Keep*, 346).

"My initial reaction was: I don't think I'm old enough. I had to do the math."

Biden referring to when he was approached by leaders of the Democratic Party in Delaware to run for the US Senate. He would only be twenty-nine years old on Election Day, when the minimum age to be senator is thirty. However, his birthday is November 20, meaning he would hit thirty between Election Day and the January date on which he would be sworn in to begin his term (*Joe Biden*, 66).

JOE'S WORLDVIEW

Democrats and Republicans each have their respective views about how foreign policy is generally to be conducted. Then there's the Biden way. Remember, this is a guy who spent much of his time as a senator serving on the Foreign Relations Committee: he should know what he's doing. We hope.

"May the hinges of our friendship never go rusty. . . . There's no doubt about them staying oiled and lubricated here [laughter in the room]. . . . Now, for those of you who are not full Irish in this room, lubricated has a different meaning for us."

Biden has shown before that he loves a good double—or even triple—entendre. He said this while welcoming Ireland's prime minister to the White House (*Daily Beast*, February 20, 2013).

VIDEO

"You know, on the way back from Mumbai to go meet with President Xi in China, I stopped in Singapore to meet with a guy named Lee Kuan Yew, who most foreign policy experts around the world say is the wisest man in the Orient."

Biden's description during a speech in Iowa of Lee Kuan Lew, founding father of modern Singapore. Someone apparently forgot to clue in Biden to the fact that the use of Orient and Oriental is widely considered outdated and offensive by Asians (ABC News, September 17, 2014).

VIDEO

"Nobody in the Senate agrees with that. Nobody in the Senate agrees with that. There is nothing to debate. He is dead, flat, unequivocally wrong."

Biden here was referring to United Nations Secretary General Kofi Annan after Annan said that military action taken without UN council approval constituted a threat to the very core of the international security system. Only the [UN] Charter provides a universally accepted legal basis for the use of force. Annan's stance closely resembled John Kerry's argument that a global test was needed for US foreign policy, meaning that it must be approved by someone else before it can be considered legitimate. Obviously Biden would disagree, putting him at odds, at least at that time, with Kerry, secretary of state as of this writing (*Surrender Is Not an Option*, 274).

"And what my constant cry was that our biggest problem is our allies—our allies in the region were our largest problem in Syria. . . . They were so determined to take down [Syrian President Bashar Hafez al-Assad] and essentially have a proxy Sunni-Shia war. What did they do? They poured hundreds of millions of dollars and tens, thousands of tons of weapons into anyone who would fight against Assad, except that the people who were being supplied were al-Nusra and al-Qaeda and the extremist elements of jihadis coming from other parts of the world."

Speaking at the Kennedy School of Government, Vice President Joe Biden was criticizing allies for supporting the same policies his administration was supporting a year earlier (*The Telegraph*, October 4, 2014).

"I said, 'Mr. Prime Minister, I'm looking into your eyes, and I don't think you have a soul.'"

A statement Biden claims to have made to Russian leader Vladimir Putin, which as of mid-2015 counts as the last time anyone in the Obama Administration made any attempt to stand up to Putin and his thuggery (*The New Yorker*, July 28, 2014).

"Your policy has been one which I fully understand— I'm not second-guessing—of one child per family."

During a Q&A in a speech at Sichuan University in Chengdu, China (*Weekly Standard*, August 21, 2011).

VIDEO

"I held hearings this year pointing out that if we do not do something of consequence about global warming, drastically and soon, we literally are going to find ourselves reconfiguring our entire military to deal with occasions for new wars, which are going to be about territory and arable land."

Biden said this early in his 2008 presidential campaign, when asked why he considered himself the strongest Democratic candidate on the issues of energy and the environment. The question posed to him mentioned nothing about fear mongering, but Biden managed to work that into his controversial answer (*Salon*, September 17, 2007).

"Kyoto is absolutely essential. The idea that we need not deal generically and nationally and internationally with global warming is absolutely ridiculous. It is maybe the single-largest long-term concern—meaning the next several decades—for the world and the United States."

More of the same, akin to the previous quote (*Salon*, September 17, 2007).

"If I could wave a wand and the Lord said I could solve one problem, I would solve the energy crisis. That's the single-most consequential problem we can solve. It's what you have to do to get greenhouse gases under control."

Shudder at the thought of any liberal Democrat brandishing a magic wand, although Biden does score points here for even acknowledging there's a lord (*Salon*, September 17, 2007).

"I am very optimistic about—about Iraq. I mean, this could be one of the great achievements of this administration. You're going to see ninety thousand American troops come marching home by the end of the summer. You're going to see a stable government in Iraq that is actually moving toward a representative government."

During a 2010 interview with then CNN host Larry King. Five years later, we've still got plenty of work to be done there, Joe (*Weekly Standard*, June 12, 2014).

VIDEO

"One thing is clear: these weapons must be dislodged from Saddam [Hussein], or Saddam must be dislodged from power."

Spoken years before all the politically induced second-guessing started kicking in (ontheissues.org). Biden said this while being interviewed by Tim Russert on *Meet the Press*'s "Meet the Candidates 2008" series, which aired September 9, 2007.

"'Well, Mr. Chancellor,' I told him, 'we can't mess up this world any more than your generation has.'"

A much younger Biden, newly named to the Foreign Relations Committee, responding to German chancellor Helmut Schmidt after Schmidt gently chastised him for being late for their meeting. Schmidt responded, "It's no wonder the world is in such bad shape. You young people don't know anything" (*Joe Biden*, 318).

"Look, Barack understood that the search for Bin Laden was about a lot more than taking a monstrous leader off the battlefield. It was about more than that. It was about righting an unspeakable wrong. Literally, it was about healing an unbearable wound—a nearly unbearable wound in America's heart. And he also knew—he also knew the message we had to send around the world. If you attack innocent Americans, we will follow you to the end of the earth!"

So what's been done about stopping terrorism since then, such as when ISIS started beheading westerners, including Americans, in 2014? Biden made this statement during his speech at the 2012 Democratic National Convention (*The Atlantic*, September 7, 2012).

"The affirmative task we have now is to actually create a new world order, because the global order is changing again. And the institutions of the world worked so well in the post-World War II era for decades, they need to be strengthened, and some have to be changed."

Notice the mention of new world order, which implies that nations including the United States would forfeit their autonomy and be subjected to rule by an international consortium. Biden mentioned this during his keynote address at the Export-Import Bank Conference in Washington, DC, in April 2013, saying a new world order would be for the sake of the worldwide economy and international business relations. Biden has emphasized the new world order theme in other speeches of his, such as when he gave the graduation address at the US Air Force Academy in May 2014. Obviously, this is scary stuff. Be afraid; be very afraid (*Examiner*, April 6, 2013).

VIDEO

KEEPING IT IN THE FAMILY

Biden has long been fond of interjecting family-inspired wisdom into his speeches, occasionally quoting his dad or his mom, or his grandfather or a favorite uncle, or . . .

"Even the oil companies don't need an incentive of $4 billion to go out and explore. As my grandpop would say, 'They're doing just fine, thank you.'"

During a speech given at a conference of the National Association of Black Journalists (*Politico*, June 20, 2012)

"My father used to have an expression. He'd say, 'Joey, a job is about a lot more than a paycheck. It's about your dignity. It's about respect. It's about your place in your community.'"

A quote from a speech Biden gave at the 2014 Global Entrepreneurship Summit in Marrakech, Morocco (whitehouse. gov, November 20, 2014).

"My parents never hit us. … All they had to say was, 'I'm so disappointed,' and that was like a knife through you."

(*Joe Biden*, 16)

"You know, folks, my dad used to have an expression. He'd say, 'A father knows he's a success when he turns and looks at his son or daughter and knows that they turned out better than he did.' I'm a success; I'm a hell of a success."

An obviously puffed-up Biden during his vice-presidential acceptance speech at the 2008 Democratic National Convention (*New York Times*, August 27, 2008).

"We had an expression in our family that you can never say anything that's true about someone when you're criticizing them. You can say you're a jerk, but you can't say, if you're three hundred pounds, you're fat. You can't say, if you're five foot three, you're a runt—you just can't say that."

(*GQ Magazine*, July 2013)

"My grandpop used to say—from Scranton—he said, 'Joey, the guy in Dunmore, the next town over . . . when the guy in Dunmore is out of work it's an economic slowdown. When your brother-in-law is out of work it's a recession. When you're out of work, it's a depression.' It's a depression for millions and millions of Americans. It's a depression."

Going off message in a Dubuque, Iowa, campaign stop in 2012 (MSNBC, June 27, 2012).

VIDEO

"My mother's creed is the American creed: 'No one is better than you. You are everyone's equal, and everyone is equal to you.'"

(*New York Times*, January 8, 2010)

"That's how I was raised. I would never greet you in this house in a way—it has nothing to do with being vice president—I would never greet you in this house without offering you something to drink. Making sure that the house was clean. Making sure that I acted like a gentleman."

(*GQ Magazine*, July 2013)

"My dad used to have an expression: 'Don't tell me what you value. Show me your budget, and I'll tell you what you value.'"

(*New York Times*, September 15, 2008)

"My dad used to have an expression: 'It is the lucky person who gets up in the morning, puts both feet on the floor, knows what they are about to do, and thinks it still matters.' I think this stuff really matters."

(CNN, November 3, 2014)

"If you get knocked down, get up."

Biden quoting his dad, Joe Biden Sr. (*Joe Biden,* 109).

"You just have to be open to the good and the bad that comes to you."

What their mom, Jean, would say, according to Valerie, Biden's sister (*Joe Biden,* 239).

"Never put another man in a corner where the only way out is over you."

Biden again quoting his dad, (*Joe Biden,* 456).

"Tell them what you really think, Joey. Let the chips fall where they may."

Grandpop Finnegan's first principle, according to Biden, referring to his maternal grandfather (*Promises to Keep,* 65).

"The world dropped you on your head? My dad would say, 'Get up! You're lying in bed feeling sorry for yourself? Get up! You got knocked on your ass on the football field? Get up! Bad grade? Get up! The girl's parents won't let her go out with a Catholic boy? Get up!'"

(*Promises to Keep,* xxii)

"'Joey you're so handsome. Joey, you're such a good athlete. Joey, you've got such a high IQ. You've got so much to say, honey, that your brain gets ahead of you.'"

Biden, quoting his mom, when she was encouraging him to work through his stuttering problem as a child (*Promises to Keep*, 5).

"You've got to be a college man."

A line that Biden said his dad sometimes used with him after having never gotten a college degree himself. (*Promises to Keep*, 16).

"Vulgarity is a sign of a limited mind trying to express itself, Joey. Why don't you come up with something more creative in trying to express your displeasure?"

This one is courtesy of Uncle Boo-Boo (Edward Blewitt "Boo-Boo" Finnegan, his mom's brother). Boo-Boo, like Joe, also had a stuttering problem. "He said this when he heard Jimmy or me using curse words we'd picked up at school," Biden said, referring to his brother (*Promises to Keep*, 21).

MISCELLANEOUS JOE

BENDING THE TRUTH

"What they didn't tell you is that the plan they've put down on paper would immediately cut benefits to more than thirty million seniors already on Medicare. What they didn't tell you is the plan they're proposing would cause Medicare to go bankrupt by 2016."

This is the kind of nonsense Biden was dishing during the 2012 presidential campaign, trying to mislead people into believing that's what would happen if a Medicare plan being floated by Republican vice presidential nominee Paul Ryan was enacted. Biden simply was wrong. The consequences he was referring to would have been the possible result of Obamacare being repealed, which was not part of Ryan's plan (AP, September 6, 2012).

EARTH DAY

"And a happy almost Earth Day to all of you. I say that because tomorrow is actually the day that officially marks the occasion. But the truth is we're here kicking off an entire Earth Week. And I hope our administration has kicked off an entire Earth administration."

Maybe we can bring back Woodstock, hippie beads and flowers in our hair while we're at it. Spare us. Biden said this while announcing funding for retrofitted homes on the eve of Earth Day, Washington, DC (*Slate*, April 21, 2010).

FAMILY

"My mom is ninety-two. She lives with me. But she's an Irish Catholic, and she thought if she wasn't a Democrat, she'd go to hell. I don't believe that, but, you know, where she comes from, to be Irish was to be Catholic, was to be a Democrat. Scranton, Pennsylvania."

At a rally for New Jersey governor Jon Corzine, Biden was explaining his mom's influence on his Democratic Party loyalty (*Slate*, October 19, 2009). Jean Biden passed away in 2010.

HYPOCRITICAL JOE

"As long as I have served, I've never seen, as my uncle once said, the Constitution stood on its head as they've done. This is the first time every single solitary decision has required sixty senators. No democracy has survived needing a supermajority."

Essentially, Biden, speaking at a fundraising event in Florida, was decrying the Republican use of the filibuster to block key Democratic initiatives in the US Senate. The part Biden leaves out is those thirty-six years he served in the US Senate, demonstrating full support of filibusters as a means to obstruct Republican presidential appointments and legislative initiatives (*Politico*, January 18, 2010; analysis includes material from Peter Roff's Thomas Jefferson Street blog at usnews.com January 19, 2010).

GLOBAL WARMING/CLIMATE CHANGE

"I think it's close to mindless. I think it's like, you know, almost like denying gravity now,"

Biden's counter when told that James Inhofe, chairman of the Senate Environment and Public Works Committee had termed climate change "the greatest hoax" perpetrated on mankind (*The Hill*, March 6, 2015).

"The willing suspension of disbelief can only be sustained so long. The expression my dad used to always use is 'Reality has a way of intruding.'"

Reality together with Biden's thought process when in public? Not exactly peas and carrots (*The Hill*, March 6, 2015).

"When the financial institutions of America began to price in the cost of carbon for the cost of doing business, you know it's reality."

(*The Hill*, March 6, 2015)

JOE COOL

"And folks, I tell you what. It was worth the trip to hear my wife say what I've never heard her say before. She's always loved me. If that's the case, why in the heck did it take five times of asking you? And that is true. Five times. I don't know what I would have done, kiddo, had you on that fifth time said no. I love you. You're the love of my life and the life of my love."

Talking about Jill, his second wife, during his acceptance speech at the 2012 Democratic National Convention (vicepresidents.com, September 7, 2012).

VIDEO

"For thirty-four years, my dad managed dealerships in Delaware. . . . I still have my 1967 Goodwood-green Corvette 327, 350-horse, with a rear-axle ratio that really gets up and goes. The Secret Service won't let me drive it. I'm not allowed to drive anything. It's the one thing I hate about this job. I'm serious."

(*Car and Driver*, October 2011)

JOE THE REALIST

"The bottom line is that no one in the country knows me. They know Joe Biden if they watch Sunday morning shows or occasionally turn on C-SPAN. But absent that, they don't know much about me at all."

Biden bemoaning the fact that headed into the 2008 primaries, he was getting only 5 percent of the vote in polls (*Joe Biden*, 384).

"I must not disguise myself from the truth. I am definitely approaching old age. My mind resents this and almost rebels, for I still feel so young, eager, agile, and alert. But one look in the mirror disillusions me. This is the season of maturity."

(*Politico*, March/April 2014)

MACHO JOE

"I'd rather be at home making love to my wife while my children are asleep."

Better than while the kids are awake, huh? Spoken during a speech in Washington, DC, to young supporters at his leadership PAC. This was in 2006, before he changed his mind and decided to go ahead and run in the 2008 presidential election, although that didn't really get anywhere. (*Slate*, June 22, 2006).

"You should always marry into a family of sisters, because it guarantees at any one time at least one of them loves you."

Biden's second wife, Jill, has four sisters (*GQ*, December 2010).

"Damn it, I want to go in."

A defiant Biden to a uniformed Capitol police officer on 9/11. The officer was yelling at the then-senator to evacuate the area. Biden wanted to go inside the Capitol despite warnings that a fourth hijacked plane was apparently headed in the direction (*Promises to Keep*, 301).

"I don't have to take this crap from you."

Biden during his first run for the US Senate speaking for the first time to Nordy Hoffman, head of Delaware's Democratic Senatorial Campaign Committee. Hoffman admitted grilling Biden during that first meeting, purposely testing Biden's mettle by asking him questions about his fitness to run and why he thought he could win the race (*Joe Biden*, 79).

"I'm not a 'keep 'em barefoot and pregnant' man, but I am all for keeping them pregnant until I have a little girl. . . . The only good thing in the world is kids."

Biden, talking about getting his start in politics while in his twenties. His first wife Neilia wanted to help him campaign, although as a family man he preferred her home with their kids. This was soon after he was elected to the New Castle County Council (*Joe Biden*, 60).

"I know I'm not supposed to like muscle cars, but I like muscle cars."

(*New York Times*, September 19, 2008)

MACHO JOE

"We take care of those who are grieving. And when that's finished they [those responsible for the killings] should know we will follow them to the gates of hell until they are brought to justice because hell is where they'll reside."

Biden talking tough in terms of going after Osama Bin Laden and the rest of al-Qaeda (*Christian Science Monitor*, September 3, 2014).

"I am so sick and tired of this pontificating about us not being the party of faith."

Biden referring to his Roman Catholic faith and the fact he had been serving in the Senate since the Nixon administration (*Cincinnati Enquirer*, 2005).

"I have seen more Romney ads about how he's going to get tough on China. To use President Clinton's phrase, in another context, 'That takes a lot of brass.'"

(*The Hill*, October 29, 2012)

"All I know is I've been looking for a fight. It's been like, 'Go ahead, smack me, give me a reason to let go.'"

Talking about the anger he felt in the aftermath of the tragic deaths of his first wife, Neilia, and their daughter, Naomi, in an auto accident just before Christmas 1972, only about a month after he had won his first senatorial race (*Joe Biden*, 110).

OBAMA

"We're not going anywhere. And you've got a homeboy in the deal who gets it."

Biden referring to his boss, President Obama, while talking to Hurricane Sandy victims (*Weekly Standard*, November 18, 2012).

"We're the ultimate odd couple. We make up for each other's shortcomings."

(*Rolling Stone*, May 9, 2013)

"Can any one of you tell me an easy way to wean ourselves off [foreign energy] dependence? Can any of you tell me a way to do that without someone being a loser? If you know that, tell me, because I will join Barack as a Nobel Laureate. Matter of fact, I kind of wondered why I wasn't. That's a joke. That's a joke. That's a joke. Only kidding. Only kidding."

Poking fun at the Nobel Committee's surprise decision to award President Obama the 2009 Nobel Peace Prize soon after he was sworn in as president. Biden had plenty of company in ridiculing Obama's selection for the Nobel (*Slate*, November 23, 2009).

"This man has courage in his soul, compassion in his heart, and a spine of steel."

Well, what would you expect Biden to say about his boss? Spoken during his acceptance speech at the 2012 Democratic National Convention (vice-presidents.com, September 7, 2012).

OVER-THE-TOP JOE

"One hundred sixty-one thousand brothers, sisters, mothers, fathers, sons, daughters, grandparents lost."

Biden overstating the number of lives lost by a factor of a thousand during the major tornado that hit Joplin, Missouri, in 2011 (*Weekly Standard*, October 3, 2014).

VIDEO

"You can go back five hundred years. You cannot find a more audacious plan. Never knowing for certain. We never had more than a 48 percent probability that [bin Laden] was there. Do any one of you have a doubt that if that raid failed that [Obama] would be a one-term president?"

Speaking at a March 2012 fundraiser in Morris Township, New Jersey, suggesting that the successful mission to kill Bin Laden was more audacious than D-Day, or anything in the Civil War or Revolutionary War (*Politico*, June 12, 2013).

"Oh my God, I'm going to get killed!"

Biden's reaction when told by then-twenty-two-year-old pollster Patrick Caddell that he would get crushed in his 1972 senate run against incumbent Cale Boggs. Biden ended up winning (*Joe Biden*, 71).

"As you probably know, some American politicians and American journalists refer to Washington, DC as the 'capital of the free world.' But it seems to me that this great city [Brussels], which boasts one thousand years of history and which serves as the capital of Belgium, the home of the European Union, and the headquarters for NATO, this city has its own legitimate claim to that title."

(FoxNews.com, May 25, 2010)

POLITICS
"People ask if I can compete with the money of Hillary and Barack. I hope at the end of the day, they can compete with my ideas and my experience."

In other words, Joe, you haven't raised much money and don't have a snowball's chance in the 2008 presidential race, right? That's what we thought (AP, January 31, 2007).

PROMISES TO BREAK

"We have no intention of downsizing the American dream."

Biden addressing class warfare going on in the political trenches while speaking at the 2012 Democratic National Convention (vicepresidents.com, September 7, 2012).

"I can make absolutely two commitments to you and all the American people tonight. One, we will find and bring to justice the men who did this. And secondly, we will get to the bottom of it. And wherever the facts lead us, wherever they lead us, we will make clear to the American public because whatever mistakes were made will not be made again."

During the 2012 vice-presidential debate with Paul Ryan, promising retribution for the terrorists who struck the American embassy in Benghazi, Libya, killing four Americans. We're still waiting (*USA Today*, August 14, 2012).

QUOTABLE JOE

"'It's not that Christianity has been tried and found wanting; it's been found difficult and left untried.'"

In comparing Christianity to the Middle East peace process, Biden was attempting to exercise his intellectual and theological muscles by quoting a line from G. K. Chesterton. Nice try. However, his audience was the American Israel Public Affairs Committee. Swing and a miss (weeklystandard. com, December 21, 2009).

"And as that bridge as you go over on Amtrak into New York through Newark, says, 'Newark makes what the world takes.' We ain't making what the world takes."

With Biden having grown up in Pennsylvania and then Delaware, this was practically local knowledge for him. Yet he needed to get his facts straight about the bridge—he was wrong. The bridge actually crosses from Pennsylvania into New Jersey, and it says: "Trenton Makes, The World Takes" (weeklystandard.com, December 21, 2009).

"I think one of the reasons we're in trouble is we reduce the political discussion to sound bites. The American public's a lot more sophisticated than we all give them credit for. And on complicated issues, I'm going to give them straight answers. And if it takes more than three minutes, I'm going to do it."

(*Joe Biden*, 378.)

"I found it unusual that someone would think, 'God, Biden was humorous.'"

Biden looking back on the time he gave his classic one-word answer in the 2008 Democratic presidential debate in which he said simply "Yes" when moderator Brian Williams asked if he could control his verbosity. The audience laughed and applauded at his answer (*Joe Biden*, 380).

SPORTS METAPHORS & MENTIONS

"The one thing I want my kids to remember about me is that I was an athlete. The hell with the rest of this stuff."

(*People Magazine*, August 25, 2008)

"There's pace on the ball."

One of Biden's pet sayings. This one refers to when things are going well for him, such as during a favorable campaign trip (*Promises to Keep*, 150).

"It's great to be back in, as my wife refers to it, Phillies-town. Once you marry an obnoxious Phillies fan like my wife—God, she is insufferable."

Referring to his wife Jill while endearing himself to Philadelphians in a 2009 speech at the Committee of Seventy's annual breakfast (*Slate*, November 23, 2009).

"You ever see me rope-a-dope?"

Biden aptly describing to reporters what his strategy would be in his 2012 vice presidential debate with Republican Paul Ryan (*Weekly Standard*, October 11, 2012).

"It's like watching gazelles."

Describing his favorite sport, women's lacrosse, at an event announcing the administration's efforts to strengthen Title IX (*Slate*, April 20, 2010).

"It's not just whether your mother can beat you in basketball that gets you excited about this. It's when you have, and you're surrounded by women who are as competitive, smarter, as smart, tough, as tough, tougher—I mean, it's an amazing thing."

Describing why men should be excited about the administration's strengthening of Title IX (*Slate*, April 20, 2010).

"I've made more than twelve thousand votes in the Senate, and there are plenty of political handicappers who, like baseball statisticians, could parse the votes, run the numbers, and make a profile of my career."

(*Promises to Keep*, 237)

"Don't throw them out, they're worth money. . . . All kidding aside, these are worth more money than you can possibly imagine."

When visiting families in Scranton whose homes had been damaged by flooding in 2011, Biden met two elderly sisters who had placed boxes and albums full of Topps baseball cards on the sidewalk to be hauled away as trash. The sisters kept the cards at his urging (*Washington Post*, August 23, 2013).

SPORTS METAPHORS & MENTIONS

"I'm so old; I played the first game ever played on this field. I didn't actually play, but I was still here."

Reminiscing at Scranton's Green Ridge Little League Field while meeting with the city's Green Ridge All-Star team in 2012. He signed baseballs and told them a little local history, explaining that he had actually sat on the bench for the historic game (*Washington Post*, August 23, 2013).

"The only question about judges is, 'Do they have good eyesight or not?' They don't get to change the strike zone. They don't get to say that was down around the ankles, you know, and I think it was a strike. They don't get to do that."

Weighing in on the 2005 confirmation hearings for Supreme Court nominee John Roberts. After learning that Roberts loved baseball, Biden would occasionally sprinkle in baseball references to his speech (*Joe Biden*, 367).

"I'm not exploring. I'm in. And this is the beginning of a marathon."

Opting against setting up an "exploratory committee" and instead entering the race directly after announcing his candidacy for the 2008 Democratic presidential nomination (ABC News, January 30, 2007)

STRETCHING THE TRUTH

"You know, I was telling the—I was telling the president, he and his country have made me look very good. I argued very, very strongly that Romania be admitted into NATO on the first round, as you'll remember. I was—and I tried to the very end as chairman of the foreign relations committee. Now look how smart I was."

Actually, Jesse Helms was chairman of the Senate Foreign Relations Committee during the first round of NATO expansion in 1999. Richard Lugar held the post when Romania was admitted in 2004 (*Weekly Standard*, December 21, 2009).

TRUTH BE TOLD

"Nixon had his enemies list and President Carter has his friends list. I guess I'm on his friends list, and I don't know which is worse."

On President Jimmy Carter, a fellow Democrat, after Carter failed to support a busing bill supported by Biden and others (*Joe Biden,* 138).

"It seems to me that we should flat-out tell the American people we are worth our salt."

During a Senate floor debate explaining his support for a Senate pay raise (*Joe Biden,* 113).

TRUTH BE TOLD
"I oppose busing. It's an asinine concept."

Biden was among just a few Democrats who opposed busing during the 1970s as part of the desegregation of schools across America, including in his home state of Delaware. "Busing," he also wrote, "was a liberal train wreck, and it was tearing people apart." (*Joe Biden*, 135).

"Innovation can only occur where you can breathe free."

(*Bloomberg Business*, May 29, 2014)

"Anybody who runs for the Supreme Court or who is appointed to the Supreme Court, to be more precise, should understand: this is not Boy Scouts; it is not Cub Scouts."

Biden, during the controversial Clarence Thomas confirmation hearings, explaining the imperfect, sometimes brutal and confrontational process of selecting and vetting Supreme Court justices. (*Joe Biden*, 276).

"It's not because I have confidence in Condi to execute foreign policy. I don't. But the president is entitled to choose the people he wants to surround himself with, even if I think his views are cockamamie."

Any quote with the word cockamamie in it deserves special recognition. Biden was explaining why he gave Condoleezza Rice a tough time with his questioning during her secretary of state confirmation hearings to replace Colin Powell. In other words, he was against her before he was for her, sort of (*Joe Biden*, 362, as told to *Rolling Stone* magazine).

"I knew the answer cold . . . [but] it would have been like clubbing the family's favorite uncle."

Referring to a debate with Republican incumbent Cale Boggs during his first run for senator. Boggs, who showed up late for the debate, admitted he didn't know the specifics of a treaty mentioned in one of the debate's questions. Biden, although he knew what to say, said he backed off on his answer as well so as not to embarrass his opponent (*Joe Biden*, 84).

"I was becoming a caricature."

Biden bemoaning his treatment by the media in the wake of plagiarism charges resurrected during his 1988 presidential campaign, referring to the Neil Kinnock and law school mistakes he had made involving lack of or improper attribution. Shallow, insubstantial, and plastic were other words used by the media to describe him (*Promises to Keep*, 202).

"Mr. Kosygin, they have an expression where I come from: Don't bulls--t a bullsh---er."

To Soviet premier Alexei Kosygin when Kosygin lowballed Biden on the number of tanks the Soviets had in their military arsenal. This occurred in 1979, when Biden was part of a six-senator delegation to Moscow seeking assurance that Soviet leaders were complying with conditions newly adopted by the Senate (*Joe Biden*, 319).

"I would be honored to run with or against John McCain, because I think the country would be better off."

(*New York Times*, August 23, 2008)

TRUTH BE TOLD

"It relates less to you than it does to the office of attorney general. I think some would say . . . that I have maybe an idealistic and unrealistic view of the office of attorney general. But I think it should be occupied by a person of extraordinary stature and character."

Biden explaining why he had opposed Edward Meese's nomination by Ronald Reagan for attorney general, saying he believed that Meese was beneath the office (*Joe Biden,* 158).

"I was probably one of those phony liberals...the kind that go out of their way to be nice to a minority, and she made me realize I was making a distinction."

An emotional Biden showing uncommon transparency while eulogizing his wife Neilia at her memorial service in December 1972. She and their thirteen-month-old daughter, Naomi, were killed in an auto accident while out Christmas shopping (*Joe Biden,* 95).

"Civil rights, sir."

Biden's succinct response his first day in the Senate in 1973 when he encountered Mississippi Senator John Stennis, a proponent of segregation, who asked Biden why he had run for the Senate (*Joe Biden,* 102).

"The more people learn about them [Obama and Hillary] and how they handle the pressure, the more their support will evaporate."

Very early on in the 2008 presidential campaign, when the Democratic primary field included Biden, Obama, and Hillary Clinton (*National Journal*, January 23, 2013).

"We can call it quits and withdraw from Iraq. I think that would be a gigantic mistake. Or we can set a deadline for pulling out, which I fear will only encourage our enemies to wait us out—equally a mistake."

A rare instance of honest, Democratic clarity, spoken by Biden in 2005 when he was still a senator on the Senate Foreign Relations Committee and hadn't yet declared for the 2008 presidential race (*Town Hall*, August 29, 2008).

"In a world this dangerous, with a crisis as tough as Iraq, hard truths need to be told. Joe Biden says this war must end now."

As stated by the announcer in a Biden presidential ad that ran in 2007, after Biden declared he was running (*Town Hall*, August 29, 2008).

"Well, I have changed my mind, but I haven't changed my mind in any fundamental way."

Biden's rope-a-dope response to *Meet the Press* moderator Tim Russert, when Russert, citing Biden's preceding 2005 quote followed by the 2007 political ad, asked Biden if he had changed his mind (*Town Hall*, August 29, 2008).

WORKS CITED

Allen, Jonathan and Amie Parnes, *HRC: State Secrets and the Rebirth of Hillary Clinton*. New York: Crown Publishers, 2014.

Allen, Jonathan and John Bresnahan. "Sources: Joe Biden Likened Tea Partiers to Terrorists." *Politico,* August 1, 2011. Accessed April 15, 2015, http://www.politico.com/news/stories/0811/60421.html#ixzz3XM7Evgwt

Allen, Mike. "Biden to Limit Role of Vice President." *Politico,* December 6, 2008. Accessed May 6, 2015, http://www.politico.com/news/stories/1208/16261.html

Ashtari, Shadee and Nick Wing. "14 Times Joe Biden Was so Joe Biden." *Huffington Post,* November 8, 2013. Accessed April 14, 2015, http://www.huffingtonpost.com/2013/11/08/thats-so-biden_n_4241176.html

Bailey, Holly. "Joe Biden, White House Truth Teller." *Newsweek,* October 9, 2009. Accessed April 14, 2015, http://www.newsweek.com/joe-biden-white-house-truth-teller-81181

Ball, Molly. "Biden: Fractured GOP Is the Problem." *The Atlantic,* October 6, 2011. Accessed April 15, 2015, http://www.theatlantic.com/politics/archive/2011/10/biden-fractured-gop-is-the-problem/246271/

Ballasy, Nicholas. "Biden Attacks Romney, Santorum, and Gingrich for Wanting 'No Rules.'" *Daily Caller,* March 15, 2012. Accessed April 14, 2015, http://dailycaller.com/2012/03/15/biden-attacks-romney-santorum-and-gingrich-for-wanting-no-rules-video/#ooid=5pbXUyNDrd7pqzzArEzGT3PDdfhEdN0o

Bannister, Craig. "Biden Declares China Part of North America." cnsnews.com, October 3, 2014. Accessed April 15, 2015, http://cnsnews.com/mrctv-blog/craig-bannister/biden-declares-china-part-north-america-0

"Biden: Avoid Planes, Trains, Automobiles." Fox News, April 30, 2009. Accessed April 10, 2015, http://www.foxnews.com/politics/2009/04/30/biden-avoid-planes-trains-automobiles/

"Biden Calls Custard Shop Manager a 'Smartass' After Taxes Comment." foxnews.com, June 27, 2010. Accessed April 13, 2015, http://www.foxnews.com/politics/2010/06/27/biden-calls-custard-shop-manager-smartass-taxes-comment/

Biden, Joe. *Promises to Keep: On Life and Politics*. New York: Random House, 2008.

"Biden Jokes that Donor Audience Was 'Dull as Hell.'" *New York Post,* April 27, 2012. Accessed April 10, 2015, http://nypost.com/2012/04/27/biden-jokes-that-donor-audience-was-dull-as-hell/

"Biden Officially Running for President." nbcnews.com/Associated Press, January 31, 2007. Accessed April 15, 2015, http://www.nbcnews.com/id/16901147/#.VS7mCfnF-So

"Biden Says Brussels Could Be 'Capital of the Free World.'" foxnews.com, May 25, 2010. Accessed April 15, 2015, http://www.foxnews.com/politics/2010/05/25/biden-says-brussels-capital-free-world/

"Biden Says Middle Class 'Buried' the Last 4 Years, Republicans Pounce." foxnews.com, October 3, 2012. Accessed April 14, 2015, http://www.foxnews.com/politics/2012/10/02/biden-says-middle-class-buried-last-4-years-republicans-pounce/

"Biden's Description of Obama Draws Scrutiny." CNN, February 9, 2007. Accessed April 14, 2015, http://www.cnn.com/2007/POLITICS/01/31/biden.obama/

"Biden's Remarks on McCain's Policies." New York Times, September 15, 2008. Accessed April 15, 2015, http://www.nytimes.com/2008/09/15/us/politics/15text-biden.html?pagewanted=all

"Biden Seeks Support in Ky." Cincinnati Enquirer, October 23, 2005. Accessed April 17, 2015, http://archive.cincinnati.com/article/20051023/NEWS0103/510230466/Biden-seeks-support-Ky-

Bohn, Kevin and Brian Rokus. "Joe Biden: I'm Not Changing." CNN, November 3, 2014. Accessed April 14, 2015, http://www.cnn.com/2014/11/03/politics/biden-not-changing-brand/

Bolton, John. Surrender Is Not an Option: Defending America at the United Nations. New York: Threshold Editions, 2008.

Boyer, Dave. "Biden's Claim of Brush with Gun Massacre Questioned." Washington Times, January 18, 2013. Accessed April 14, 2015, http://www.washingtontimes.com/news/2013/jan/18/bidens-claim-brush-gun-massacre-questioned/?page=all

Boyle, Matthew. "Biden on Cheerleaders: 'The Stuff They Do on Hard Wood, It Blows My Mind.'" Daily Caller, September 21, 2012. Accessed April 14, 2015, http://dailycaller.com/2012/09/21/biden-on-cheerleaders-the-stuff-they-do-on-hard-wood-it-blows-my-mind/

Brinkley, Douglas. "Joe Biden: The Rolling Stone Interview." Rolling Stone, May 23, 2013. Accessed April 15, 2015, http://www.rollingstone.com/politics/news/joe-biden-the-rolling-stone-interview-20130509

Broder, John M. "Father's Tough Life an Inspiration for Biden." New York Times, October 24, 2008. Accessed April 13, 2015, http://www.nytimes.com/2008/10/24/us/politics/24biden.html?pagewanted=all

Brouillette, Julia. "Quotes to Note: VPOTUS Joe Biden in Austin." dailytexanonline.com, October 30, 2013. Accessed April 14, 2015, http://www.dailytexanonline.com/news/2013/10/30/quotes-to-note-vpotus-joe-biden-in-austin

Buford, Talia. "Biden: 'A Gaffe Is When You Tell the Truth.'" Politico, June 20, 2012. Accessed April 14, 2015, http://www.politico.com/politico44/2012/06/biden-a-gaffe-is-when-you-tell-the-truth-126866.html

Burns, Alexander. "VP: 'Constitution on Its Head.'" *Politico*, January 18, 2010. Accessed April 15, 2015, http://www.politico.com/politico44/perm/0110/biden_slams_filibuster_fe40df44-9045-4c26-a715-51c427035eae.html

Burns, Alexander. "VP: 'Sleeping with a Teacher.'" *Politico*, April 27, 2010. Accessed April 13, 2015, http://www.politico.com/politico44/perm/0410/pillow_talk_92217e5a-2429-4aaf-a406-8d4e88a8afd5.html

Byrd, Lorie. "A Snapshot of Joe Biden's Foreign Policy Judgment." *Town Hall*, August 29, 2008. Accessed April 15, 2015, http://townhall.com/columnists/loriebyrd/2008/08/29/a_snapshot_of_joe_bidens_foreign_policy_judgment/page/full

Cama, Timothy. "Biden: Climate Skepticism 'Like Denying Gravity.'" *The Hill*, March 6, 2015. Accessed April 15, 2015, http://thehill.com/policy/energy-environment/234853-biden-climate-skepticism-like-denying-gravity

Cheney, Dick and Liz Cheney. *In My Time: A Personal and Political Memoir*. New York: Threshold Editions, 2011.

Clyne, Meghan. "A Little Learning ..." *Weekly Standard*, December 21, 2009. Accessed April 15, 2015, http://www.weeklystandard.com/Content/Public/Articles/000/000/017/332vjqsc.asp

Commission on Presidential Debates. "October 2, 2008 Debate Transcript." *Debates.org*, October 2, 2008. Accessed April 14, 2015, http://www.debates.org/index.php?page=2008-debate-transcript-2

Corsaro, Ryan. "Biden Says Hillary Might Be a Better VP." *CBS News*, September 10, 2008. Accessed April 10, 2015, http://www.cbsnews.com/news/biden-says-hillary-might-be-a-better-vp/

Crowley, Patrick. "Biden Seeks Support in Ky." *Cincinnati Enquirer*, October 23, 2005. (No link available).

Cruz, Noelia de la. "Vice President Joe Biden Addresses Gun Safety Questions in Facebook Town Hall with *Parents Magazine*." parents.com, February 19, 2013. Accessed April 14, 2015, http://www.parents.com/blogs/parents-news-now/2013/02/19/must-read/vice-president-joe-biden-addresses-gun-safety-questions-in-facebook-town-hall-with-parents-magazine/

DePaulo, Lisa. "$#!% Joe Biden Says." *GQ*, December 2010. Accessed April 15, 2015, http://www.gq.com/news-politics/politics/201012/joe-biden-interview-vice-president-obama

Dickson, Caitlin. "'Buy a Shotgun!' and More of Joe Biden's Never-Ending Gaffes." *The Daily Beast*, February 20, 2013. Accessed April 15, 2015, http://www.thedailybeast.com/articles/2012/04/26/the-never-ending-list-of-vice-president-joe-biden-s-verbal-gaffes.html

Dionne, E. J., Jr. "Biden Admits Errors and Criticizes Latest Report." *New York Times*, September 22, 1987. Accessed April 15, 2015, http://www.nytimes.com/1987/09/22/us/biden-admits-errors-and-criticizes-latest-report.html

Dionne, E. J., Jr. "Biden Joins Campaign for Presidency." *New York Times*, June 10, 1987. Accessed April 14, 2015, http://www.nytimes.com/1987/06/10/us/biden-joins-campaign-for-the-presidency.html

Draper, Robert. "Joe Biden Can't Shut Up." *GQ*, March 2006. Accessed April 15, 2015, http://www.gq.com/news-politics/newsmakers/200602/joe-biden-iraq-bush-war-democrats-republicans

Eilperin, Juliet. "The 7 Best Joe Biden Quotes from the Ed Markey Fundraiser." *Washington Post*, June 12, 2013. Accessed April 15, 2015, http://www.washingtonpost.com/blogs/the-fix/wp/2013/06/11/biden-unplugged-on-behalf-of-markeys-senate-bid/

Epstein, Jennifer. "Biden: Bin Laden Killing Most 'Audacious' Plan in 500 Years." *Politico*, March 19, 2012. Accessed April 15, 2015, http://www.politico.com/politico44/2012/03/biden-bin-laden-killing-most-audacious-plan-in-years-117961.html

"Fact Check: Biden's Chopper Was 'Forced Down' by Snowflakes." foxnews.com/Associated Press, October 2, 2008. Accessed April 14, 2015, http://www.foxnews.com/story/2008/10/02/fact-check-biden-chopper-was-forced-down-by-snowflakes/

Friedersdorf, Conor. "VP at the DNC: Joe Biden's Disturbing Riff on Killing Osama Bin Laden." *The Atlantic*, September 7, 2012. Accessed April 15, 2015, http://www.theatlantic.com/politics/archive/2012/09/vp-at-the-dnc-joe-bidens-disturbing-riff-on-killing-osama-bin-laden/262090/

Gehrke, Joel. "Biden: Republicans voted for a $500 trillion tax cut for 120,000 families." *Washington Examiner*, October 26, 2012. Accessed April 15, 2015, http://www.washingtonexaminer.com/biden-republicans-voted-for-a-500-trillion-tax-cut-for-120000-families/article/2511822

Gelb, Leslie H. "Joe Biden on Iraq, Iran, China, and the Taliban." *Newsweek*, December 19, 2011. Accessed April 14, 2015, http://www.newsweek.com/joe-biden-iraq-iran-china-and-taliban-65953

Glass, Charles. "Without Peace in Syria, the Beheadings Will Not Stop." *The Telegraph*, October 4, 2014. Accessed April 15, 2015, http://www.telegraph.co.uk/news/worldnews/middleeast/iraq/11140892/Without-peace-in-Syria-the-beheadings-will-not-stop.html

Glueck, Katie. "VP Debate 2012: Joe Biden's 5 Best Lines." *Politico*, October 11, 2012. Accessed April 14, 2015, http://www.politico.com/news/stories/1012/82319.html

Greenberg, Jon. "Sorting Out the Truth on the Attack in Libya." *Tampa Bay Times*, October 18, 2012. Accessed April 14, 2015, http://www.politifact.com/truth-o-meter/article/2012/oct/18/sorting-out-truth-attack-libya/

Grier, Peter. "Joe Biden Congratulates Wrong Guy for Boston Mayoral Win. Who Messed Up?" *Christian Science Monitor*, November 7, 2013. Accessed April 14, 2015, http://www.csmonitor.com/USA/Politics/Decoder/2013/1107/Joe-Biden-congratulates-wrong-guy-for-Boston-mayoral-win.-Who-messed-up-video

Grier, Peter. "Joe Biden Vows to Chase Islamic State to 'Gates of Hell.' Does He Mean It?" *Christian Science Monitor*, September 3, 2014. Accessed April 15, 2015, http://www.csmonitor.com/USA/Politics/Decoder/2014/0903/Joe-Biden-vows-to-chase-Islamic-State-to-gates-of-hell.-Does-he-mean-it-video

Griffin, Pete. "Biden to Union Members: If You Vote Republican, Don't Ask Me for Any Help." Fox News, published July 1, 2011. Accessed April 14, 2015, http://www.foxnews.com/politics/2011/07/01/biden-to-union-members-if-vote-republican-dont-ask-me-for-any-help/

Griscom Little, Amanda. "Joe Biden: Face Global Warming or Global Conflict." *Salon*, September 17, 2007. Accessed April 15, 2015, http://www.salon.com/2007/09/17/biden_qa/

Grossman, Samantha. "A History of Vice Presidential Picks, from the Pages of *Time*." newsfeed.time.com, August 10, 2012. Accessed April 14, 2015, http://newsfeed.time.com/2012/08/11/a-history-of-vice-presidential-picks-from-the-pages-of-time/

Hallowell, Billy. "5 of the Most Absurd Gun Comments from Joe Biden." *Blaze*, April 12, 2013. Accessed April 14, 2015, http://www.theblaze.com/stories/2013/04/12/joe-bidens-5-most-absurd-quotes-about-firearms-and-gun-owners/

Halper, Daniel. "Biden Gaffes His Way across Europe." *Weekly Standard*, February 5, 2013. Accessed April 15, 2015, http://www.weeklystandard.com/blogs/biden-gaffes-his-way-across-europe_700254.html

Halper, Daniel. "Biden Once Called Iraq One of Obama's 'Great Achievements.'" *Weekly Standard*, June 12, 2014. Accessed April 15, 2015, http://www.weeklystandard.com/blogs/biden-once-called-iraq-one-obamas-great-achievments_794909.html#

Halper, Daniel. "Biden Overstates Deaths in Joplin, Missouri Tornado by 160,839." *Weekly Standard*, October 3, 2014. Accessed April 15, 2015, http://www.weeklystandard.com/blogs/biden-overstates-deaths-joplin-missouri-tornado-160839_808538.html

Halper, Daniel. "Biden: 'Yes We Do' Want to Raise Taxes by a Trillion Dollars." *Weekly Standard*, October 4, 2012. Accessed April 14, 2015, http://www.weeklystandard.com/blogs/biden-yes-we-do-want-raise-taxes-trillion-dollars_653666.html

Halper, Daniel. "Biden Refers to Fallen Soldiers as 'Fallen Angels.'" September 7, 2012. Accessed April 10, 2015, http://www.weeklystandard.com/blogs/biden-refers-fallen-soldiers-fallen-angels_651916.html

Halper, Daniel. "Biden: 'I'm Going to Give You the Whole Load Today.'" *Weekly Standard*, October 31, 2012. Accessed April 13, 2015, http://www.weeklystandard.com/blogs/biden-im-going-give-you-whole-load-today_659899.html

Halper, Daniel. "Biden Calls Republicans 'Neanderthals.'" *Weekly Standard*, September 13, 2013. Accessed April 14, 2015, http://www.weeklystandard.com/blogs/biden-calls-republicans-neanderthals_753935.html

Halper, Daniel. "Biden: 'Folks, Where's It Written We Cannot Lead the World in the 20th Century in Making Automobiles'?" *Weekly Standard*, August 15, 2012. Accessed April 14, 2015, http://www.weeklystandard.com/blogs/biden-folks-wheres-it-written-we-cant-lead-world-20th-century_650017.html#

Halper, Daniel. "TelePrompter Trips Biden Up." *Weekly Standard*, March 21, 2014. Accessed April 14, 2015, http://www.weeklystandard.com/blogs/teleprompter-trips-biden_785725.html

Halper, Daniel. "Biden Calls Obama 'Homeboy.'" *Weekly Standard*, November 18, 2012. Accessed April 15, 2015, http://www.weeklystandard.com/blogs/biden-calls-obama-homeboy_663632.html

Halper, Daniel. "Biden: 'You Ever See Me Rope-a-Dope?'" *Weekly Standard*, October 11, 2012. Accessed April 15, 2015, http://www.weeklystandard.com/blogs/biden-you-ever-see-me-rope-dope_654202.html

Hamby, Peter. "'White Boy' Biden Calls Tea Party 'Crazy.'" CNN, October 15, 2014. Accessed April 14, 2015, http://www.cnn.com/2014/10/14/politics/biden-south-carolina/

Heil, Emily. "Did Joe Biden Confess to Ellen that He's Bored at SOTU? Or that He's Obama's Work Husband?" *Washington Post*, January 26, 2015. Accessed April 14, 2015, http://www.washingtonpost.com/blogs/reliable-source/wp/2015/01/26/did-joe-biden-confess-to-ellen-that-hes-bored-at-sotu-or-that-hes-obamas-work-husband/

Hemingway, Mark. "Joe Biden: 'I Fully Understand' China's One-Child Policy." *Weekly Standard*, August 22, 2011. Accessed April 15, 2015, http://www.weeklystandard.com/blogs/joe-biden-i-fully-understand-chinas-one-child-policy_590513.html

Horowitz, Jason. "Biden Unbound: Lays into Clinton, Obama, Edwards." *New York Observer*, February 5, 2007. Accessed April 10, 2015, http://observer.com/2007/02/biden-unbound-lays-into-clinton-obama-edwards/

Howerton, Jason. "Joe Biden to Father of Former Navy SEAL Killed in Benghazi: 'Did Your Son Always Have Balls the Size of Cue Balls?'" Blaze, October 25, 2012. Accessed April 10, 2015, http://www.theblaze.com/stories/2012/10/25/joe-biden-to-father-of-former-navy-seal-killed-in-benghazi-did-your-son-always-have-balls-the-size-of-cue-balls/

Itkowitz, Colby. "Loop Quote of the Week Winner: Joe Biden." *Washington Post*, March 21, 2014. Accessed April 13, 2015, http://www.washingtonpost.com/blogs/in-the-loop/wp/2014/03/21/loop-quote-of-the-week-winner-joe-biden/

Izadi, Elahe. "Joe Biden vs. Hillary Clinton? A Look Back at Their Last Face-off." *National Journal*, January 23, 2013. Accessed April 15, 2015, http://www.nationaljournal.com/politics/joe-biden-vs-hillary-clinton-a-look-back-at-their-last-face-off-20130123.

Jackson, David. "Biden to Crowd: Romney Will 'Put You All Back in Chains.'" *USA Today*, August 14, 2012. Accessed April 15, 2015, http://content.usatoday.com/communities/theoval/post/2012/08/biden-to-crowd-romney-will-put-you-all-back-in-chains/1#.VS7nHPnF-Sp

"Joe Being Joe." freebeacon.com, August 5, 2014. Accessed April 15, 2015, http://freebeacon.com/politics/joe-being-joe-6/

"Joe Biden Appears to Have No Idea Who Van Jones Is." *Huffington Post*, December 4, 2011. Accessed April 15, 2015, http://www.huffingtonpost.com/2011/10/04/joe-biden-van-jones-occupy-wall-street_n_994780.html

Johnson, Andrew. "Biden: 'Tea Baggers' Preventing New Gun-Control Laws." *National Review*, July 7, 2014. Accessed April 14, 2015, http://www.nationalreview.com/corner/382149/biden-tea-baggers-preventing-new-gun-control-laws-andrew-johnson

Keller, Ryan. "Vice President Joe Biden Calls for a 'New World Order.'" *Examiner*, April 6, 2013. Accessed April 15, 2015, http://www.examiner.com/article/vice-president-joe-biden-calls-for-a-new-world-order

Keller, Susan Jo. "Catherine E. F. Biden, Mother of the Vice President, Is Dead at 92." *New York Times*, January 8, 2010. Accessed April 15, 2015, http://www.nytimes.com/2010/01/09/us/politics/09biden.html

Killough, Ashley. "Biden Says Use of Term 'Shylocks' Was a Poor Choice." CNN, September 17, 2014. Accessed April 15, 2015, http://www.cnn.com/2014/09/17/politics/joe-biden-jewish-term/

Koren, Marina, "The Best Joe Biden Quotes from the Senate's First Day." *National Journal*, January 6, 2015. Accessed April 10, 2015, http://www.nationaljournal.com/congress/the-best-joe-biden-quotes-from-the-senate-s-first-day-20150106

Koski, Justin. "Watch Joe Biden Creep Out New Senators and Their Families." *Western Journalism*, January 8, 2015. Accessed on April 14, 2015, http://www.westernjournalism.com/watch-joe-biden-creep-new-senators-families/#oKAz7raUp27iACsl.99

Krieg, Gregory. "The Best of Joe Biden Being Joe Biden at Tuesday's Senate Swearing-in Ceremony." mic.com, January 6, 2015. Accessed on April 13, 2015, http://mic.com/articles/107820/the-best-of-joe-biden-being-joe-biden-at-tuesday-s-senate-swearing-in-ceremony

Kurtzman, Daniel. "Bidenisms." about.com. Accessed April 10, 2015, http://politicalhumor.about.com/od/joebiden/a/bidenisms.htm

Lapidos, Juliet. "Loin-Girding 101." *Slate*, October 21, 2008. Accessed April 14, 2015, http://www.slate.com/articles/news_and_politics/explainer/2008/10/loingirding_101.html

Larotonda, Matthew. "Biden's Awkward Sex Joke: Big Family, Thin Walls." ABC News, July 10, 2012. Accessed April 14, 2015, http://abcnews.go.com/blogs/politics/2012/07/bidens-awkward-sex-joke-big-family-thin-walls/

Laskas, Jeanne Marie. "Have You Heard the One about President Joe Biden?" *GQ*, July 2013. Accessed April 13, 2010, http://www.gq.com/news-politics/newsmakers/201308/joe-biden-presidential-campaign-2016-2013

Leibovich, Mark. "Meanwhile, the Other No. 2 Keeps on Punching." *New York Times*, September 20, 2008. Accessed on April 14, 2015, http://www.nytimes.com/2008/09/20/us/politics/20biden.html?pagewanted=print&_r=0

Lemire, Jonathan. "VP Debate: Joe Biden, Paul Ryan Lock Horns over Economy, Taxes, and Foreign Policy in Lively Debate." *New York Daily News*, October 12, 2012. Accessed April 14, 2015, http://www.nydailynews.com/news/politics/biden-ryan-lock-horns-lively-debate-article-1.1181491

"List of Biden's Political Blunders." Fox News, October 6, 2014. Accessed April 14, 2015, http://www.foxnews.com/politics/2014/10/06/bidens-list-political-blunders/

Mann, James. *The Obamians: The Struggle Inside the White House to Redefine American Power.* New York: Viking Press, 2012.

Mason, Julie. "Biden to Latinos: You Were Here First." *Politico,* September 30, 2011. Accessed April 15, 2015, http://www.politico.com/politico44/perm/0911/fiesta_7c28ea82-9f05-4ecc-bf58-a8f38e5c5f0a.html

McIntyre, Michael K. "Joe Biden Has Been Campaigning So Much He Doesn't Even Know Where He Is: Michael K. McIntyre's Tipoff." *Cleveland Plain Dealer,* November 1, 2012. Accessed April 14, 2015, http://www.cleveland.com/tipoff/index.ssf/2012/11/joe_biden_has_been_campaigning.html

Mears, Bill. "Roberts Sidesteps Questions on Pledge, Eminent Domain." CNN, September 15, 2005. Accessed April 14, 2015, http://www.cnn.com/2005/POLITICS/09/14/roberts.hearings/

Miller, Jake. "Joe Biden on Patriots' Deflation Controversy: 'I Like a Softer Ball.'" CBS News, January 21, 2015. Accessed April 15, 2015, http://www.cbsnews.com/news/joe-biden-on-patriots-deflation-controversy-i-like-a-softer-ball/

Muskal, Michael. "Political Commentary from the LA Times." *Los Angeles Times,* April 3, 2009. Accessed April 17, 2015, http://latimesblogs.latimes.com/washington/2009/04/biden-obama-overseas.html

Newby, Joe. "Joe Biden: 'I've Known Eight Presidents, Three of Them Intimately.'" *Examiner,* August 23, 2012. Accessed April 10, 2015, http://www.examiner.com/article/joe-biden-i-ve-known-eight-presidents-three-of-them-intimately

Ohlheiser, Abby. "Joe Biden Totally Joe Bidened a Line in His Boston Memorial Speech." *The Wire,* April 15, 2014. Accessed April 15, 2015, http://www.thewire.com/politics/2014/04/joe-biden-totally-joe-bidened-a-line-in-his-boston-memorial-speech/360697/

Osnos, Evan. "The Biden Agenda." *The New Yorker,* July 28, 2014. Accessed April 13, 2015, http://www.newyorker.com/magazine/2014/07/28/biden-agenda

Pazzanese, Christina. "All Politics is Personal; VP Biden Delivers Address at Kennedy School Forum." *Harvard Gazette,* October 3, 2014. Accessed April 10, 2015, http://www.hks.harvard.edu/news-events/news/articles/joe-biden-forum-event

Phillips, John. "What I'd Do Differently: Vice President Joe Biden." *Car and Driver,* October 2011. Accessed April 15, 2015, http://www.caranddriver.com/features/what-id-do-differently-vice-president-joe-biden-interview

Phillips, Kate. "McCain Rolls Out New Ad with Biden's Words." *New York Times,* August 23, 2008. Accessed April 15, 2015, http://thecaucus.blogs.nytimes.com/2008/08/23/mccain-rolls-out-new-ad-with-bidens-words/

Premiere Authors Literary Agency. *Sh*t My Vice President Says.* New York: Threshold Editions, Simon & Schuster, 2010.

"Press Briefing by the Vice President and Press Secretary Robert Gibbs, 6/17/2010." whitehouse. gov, June 17, 2010. Accessed April 14, 2015, https://www.whitehouse.gov/the-press-office/press-briefing-vice-president-and-press-secretary-robert-gibbs-6172010

"Remarks by the President and Vice President on Health Insurance Reform at the Department of the Interior." whitehouse.gov, March 23, 2010. Accessed April 14, 2015, https://www.whitehouse.gov/the-press-office/remarks-president-and-vice-president-health-insurance-reform-bill-department-interi

"Remarks by Vice President Joe Biden to the Global Entrepreneurship Summit." whitehouse. gov, November 20, 2014. Accessed April 15, 2015, https://www.whitehouse.gov/the-press-office/2014/11/20/remarks-vice-president-joe-biden-global-entrepreneurship-summit

Roberts, Dexter. "Biden Makes a Habit of Dissing Chinese Innovation." *Bloomberg Business*, May 29, 2014. Accessed April 15, 2015, http://www.bloomberg.com/bw/articles/2014-05-29/biden-makes-a-habit-of-dissing-chinese-innovation

Roff, Peter. "Joe Biden's Filibuster Hypocrisy." *US News*, January 19, 2010. Accessed April 15, 2015, http://www.usnews.com/opinion/blogs/peter-roff/2010/01/19/joe-bidens-filibuster-hypocrisy

Saenz, Arlette. "Biden Likens Republicans to 'Squealing Pigs.'" ABC News, August 21, 2012. Accessed April 14, 2015, http://abcnews.go.com/blogs/politics/2012/08/biden-likens-republicans-to-squealing-pigs/

Saenz, Arlette and Erin Dooley. "Why Today Was the Best Day Ever to Watch Biden Being Biden." ABC News, Jan 6, 2015. Accessed April 10, 2015, http://abcnews.go.com/Politics/today-best-day-watch-biden-biden/story?id=28037731

Seitz-Wald, Alex. "Joe Biden on Ben Carson: 'I Mean Jesus, God.'" MSNBC, March 6, 2015. Accessed April 14, 2015, http://www.msnbc.com/msnbc/joe-biden-ben-carson-i-mean-jesus-god

Shapiro, Ben. "This VP Stuff Is Tough." *Breitbart*, October 4, 2012. Accessed April 15, 2015, http://www.breitbart.com/big-government/2012/10/04/biden-this-vp-stuff-is-tough/

Slack, Donovan. "Biden on the 47 Percent: What Country Are Romney and Ryan Living In?" *Politico,* September 21, 2012. Accessed April 14, 2015, http://www.politico.com/politico44/2012/09/biden-on-the-percent-what-country-are-romney-and-136325.html

Spiering, Charlie. "Joe Biden Backs Park Ranger Who Stopped Vets at WWII Memorial." *Washington Examiner*, October 4, 2013. Accessed April 14, 2015, http://www.washingtonexaminer.com/joe-biden-backs-park-ranger-who-stopped-vets-at-wwii-memorial/article/2536812

Stahl, Jeremy. "The Complete Bidenisms." *Slate*, April 30, 2010. Accessed April 13, 2015, http://www.slate.com/articles/news_and_politics/bidenisms/2009/09/the_complete_bidenisms.html

Starr, Penny. "Joe Biden: 'We Have to Go Spend Money to Keep From Going Bankrupt.'" CNS News, July 16, 2009. Accessed April 10, 2015, http://cnsnews.com/news/article/joe-biden-we-have-go-spend-money-keep-going-bankrupt

Steyn, Mark. "A Citizen-Politician Runs for Veep." *National Review*, October 4, 2008. Accessed April 14, 2015, http://www.nationalreview.com/article/225882/wink-and-smile-mark-steyn

Strauss, Daniel. "Bill Clinton: Mitt Romney's Jeep-to-China Ad Is 'Biggest Load of Bull in the World.'" thehill.com, October 29, 2012. Accessed April 15, 2015, http://thehill.com/video/campaign/264725-bill-clinton-romneys-jeep-ad-is-biggest-load-of-bull-in-the-world

Sullivan, Sean. "Biden: Romney's Approach to Financial Regulation Will 'Put Y'all Back in Chains.'" *Washington Post*, August 14, 2012. Accessed April 10, 2015, http://www.washingtonpost.com/blogs/the-fix/wp/2012/08/14/biden-romneys-approach-to-financial-regulation-will-put-you-all-back-in-chains/

Tam, Ruth. "Joe Biden's Top Scranton Moments." *Washington Post*, August 23, 2013. Accessed April 15, 2015, http://www.washingtonpost.com/blogs/the-fix/wp/2013/08/23/joe-bidens-top-scranton-moments/

"Text of Joe Biden's Statement on Senators' Letter to Iran's Leaders." *Wall Street Journal*, March 9, 2015. Accessed April 15, 2015, http://blogs.wsj.com/washwire/2015/03/09/text-of-joe-bidens-statement-on-senators-letter-to-irans-leaders/

Thai, Xuan and Ted Barrett. "Biden's Description of Obama Draws Scrutiny." CNN, February 9, 2007. Accessed April 15, 2015, http://www.cnn.com/2007/POLITICS/01/31/biden.obama/

Thrush, Glenn. "Joe Biden in Winter." *Politico*, March/April 2014. Accessed April 13, 2015, http://www.politico.com/magazine/story/2014/02/joe-biden-profile-103667_full.html#.VSyiZPnF-So

"Top 10 Joe Biden Gaffes" *Time*. Accessed April 10, 2015, http://content.time.com/time/specials/packages/completelist/0,29569,1895156,00.html

Torres, Alec. "Biden: Obama and I Aren't 'Technology Geeks,' Thought Website Would Be Fine." *National Review*, October 31, 2013. Accessed April 14, 2015, http://www.nationalreview.com/corner/362722/biden-obama-and-i-arent-technology-geeks-thought-website-would-be-fine-alec-torres

"Transcript of the Third Democratic Primary Presidential Debate." *New York Times*, June 28, 2007. Accessed April 14, 2015, http://www.nytimes.com/2007/06/28/us/politics/29transcript.html?pagewanted=all&_r=0

Travers, Karen. "Biden Says White House Getting Earful from Nervous Lawmakers over Health Care." ABC News, March 18, 2010. Accessed April 14, 2015, http://abcnews.go.com/Nightline/Politics/vice-president-joe-biden-tells-abc-exclusive-passing/story?id=10139848

Trudeau, G. B. *Doonesbury.com's The War in Quotes*. Kansas City, MO: Andrews McMeel Publishing, 2008.

"Unmitigated Buffoonery: Joe Biden Harkens Teddy Roosevelt, Refers to Illegal Immigrants as 'American Citizens.'" glennbeck.com, March 28, 2014. Access April 14, 2015, http://www.glennbeck.com/2014/03/28/unmitigated-buffoonery-joe-biden-harkens-teddy-roosevelt-refers-to-illegal-immigrants-as-american-citizens/?utm_source=glennbeck&utm_medium=contentcopy_link

"VP Goes Full Biden for Senate Swearing-in Ceremony." NBC News, January 6, 2015. Accessed April 14, 2015, http://www.nbcnews.com/politics/first-read/vp-goes-full-biden-senate-swearing-ceremony-n280921

Venezia, Todd. "Biden Gives a Shout Out to His Butt Buddy." *New York Post*, February 12, 2015. Accessed April 13, 2015, http://nypost.com/2015/02/12/biden-gives-a-shout-out-to-his-butt-buddy/

Walshe, Shushannah. "Joe Biden Refers to Asia as 'The Orient.'" ABC News, September 17, 2014. Accessed April 15, 2015, http://abcnews.go.com/blogs/politics/2014/09/joe-biden-refers-to-asia-as-the-orient/

Welch, Matt. "When Joe Biden Loved Defying the President's Foreign Policy." reason.com, March 10, 2015. Accessed April 15, 2015, http://reason.com/blog/2015/03/10/when-joe-biden-loved-defying-the-preside

Westfall, Sandra Sobieraj. "Barack Obama Reveals How He Popped the Question to Joe Biden." *People*, August 25, 2008. Accessed April 15, 2015, http://www.people.com/people/article/0,,20221223_2,00.html

Witcover, Jules, *Joe Biden: A Life of Trial and Redemption*. New York: HarperCollins, 2010.

Woodward, Calvin and Tom Raum. "Fact Check: Biden on Jobs and Medicare." Associated Press, September 6, 2012. Accessed April 15, 2015, http://news.yahoo.com/fact-check-biden-jobs-medicare-023147199--election.html

York, Byron. "Biden: 'I Don't Want Real Job ... You Have to Produce.'" *Washington Examiner*, March 30, 2012. Accessed April 13, 2015, http://www.washingtonexaminer.com/biden-i-dont-want-real-jobyou-have-to-produce/article/1205066

Zezima, Katie. "Joe Biden Said He Has 'No Savings Accounts.'" *Washington Post*, June 23, 2014. Accessed April 14, 2015, http://www.washingtonpost.com/blogs/post-politics/wp/2014/06/23/joe-biden-said-he-has-no-savings-accounts/

ACKNOWLEDGMENTS

Thanks to WND Books and editorial director Geoffrey Stone for giving me the opportunity to expand my horizons and exercise some of my political chops in editing this book. I had a good team around me at WND, with helping hands from creative director Mark Karis, production editor Kelsey Whited, video guru Conrad Tice, and marketing coordinator Michael Thompson. As always, thank you, Holley and Andrew, for always standing by while I sequestered myself for weeks on end researching this book. Thanks, too, to our Lord Jesus Christ, who's unceasingly present when I need Him and even when I dare think I don't.

ABOUT THE AUTHOR

The seriously conservative yet politically independent Mike Towle is the Tennessee-based founder and president of Win-Win Words, LLC, a firm offering a variety of contract services to include corporate communications, content creation for publication, and self-publishing consultation. He is also the author of more than a dozen other published books, including works on the likes of Pat Tillman, Ben Hogan, Roger Staubach, Walter Payton, Pete Rose, Vince Lombardi, Arthur Ashe, and Ara Parseghian. Towle is a former newspaper reporter, editor, columnist, and sports writer for the *Vermont Sunday News, Fort Worth Star-Telegram, National,* and *Tennessean,* as well as a contributing writer for several golf publications. Towle also has served stints as a book editor for several publishers, including Rutledge Hill Press and TowleHouse Publishing. A native of Vermont, a graduate of the University of Notre Dame and a longtime Texas resident, Towle now resides in Hendersonville, Tennessee, with his wife Holley and son Andrew, an Eagle Scout.